"Once again, Jim Bohn, Ph.D., has given us what most others can't, a "how to" book based on real world experience. Unlike many others, Jim comes with an infrastructure built over many years of relatable experience and complementary education. I caution our membership on reading a book and then thinking they can implement the "perfect world" the author promises; however, "perfect world" and "real world" can be parallel universes that never meet. Jim brings the real world approach and honest insight into what it takes to be a successful leader today. His new book delivers the "nuts and bolts" of what leaders need to know and do. He layers his book with "cut to the chase" insights on how to develop yourself, your team, and integrate these strategies into the organization's success. Jim's new book is refreshing and thought provoking.

Linda G. Kiedrowski, CEO
The Paranet Group, Inc.

"Great, clear, and easily applicable leadership information. Easy to read and apply to daily leadership challenges and opportunities—I enjoyed reading this very much. I read it on the plane; it totally made sense, and also gave me pause to rethink some of my approaches."

Deborah Roberts, Senior Vice President—Healthcare
Sodexho

"Aspiring leaders; frustrated leaders; coaching leaders working to develop the next generation will all appreciate the many great lessons and clear instructions provided in this book. Dr. Jim Bohn is *not* an academic writing about leadership theory developed in a classroom; he is the type of proven, hands-on, no nonsense leader that has learned in the field for decades, and he has a unique gift for sharing his insight in a clear, actionable format."

Dean Atchison
Spectrum Aeromed

"Jim Bohn came to our organization highly recommended, and we were thrilled that he could bring his leadership training skills to our area nonprofit leaders. I highly recommend *The Nuts and Bolts of Leadership* as a must read for busy nonprofit leadership teams. Community leaders' list of things to accomplish in one day is overwhelming, but Jim reminds us to take time; time for the visioning process that is imperative for our organizations to, using his analogy, climb to the top. In his new book, Jim once again delivers unique insights and common sense wisdom in a quick how-to book to help leaders reach that next level."

Brenda Peterson, Executive Director
Volunteer Center, Ozaukee County

DEDICATION

As the title of this book indicates, Leadership is about getting the job done. Throughout my work life I have been impressed, educated, inspired, and coached by some of the finest leaders in the world. I look back over my early career and recognize the influence of many, but some who I must mention here.

In my early career on the drafting board, I met a most insightful and interesting leader, Ken Jones, who ran the Engineering Group at Globe Union. He challenged me day and night to try new things and coached, encouraged and inspired me to push hard to get things done. "Always be going somewhere – don't waste time." He modeled that for me.

Terry Weaver was the most focused leader I ever worked with; the man knew what he wanted to accomplish, and he helped us launch one of the flagship products of Johnson Controls.

Later on, I had opportunities to work with some exceptional leaders at Johnson Controls. Betty Arndt comes to mind; she was poised, polished, and professional, and taught me about my own personal "brand." She was, perhaps, one of the most amazing people I ever worked with, and she changed our organization for the good.

Deborah Roberts stands out as a leader who gave me such good advice and coaching in my sales career, and she was always interested in finding new and interesting ways to solve customer problems (and she didn't mind singing with me at a piano -- great voice!).

Iain Campbell was a powerhouse of a leader with a soaring intellect. I have never met a leader who could speak with such depth on so many subjects. He was incredible.

Jim Hanson demonstrated outstanding persistence in the face of unimaginable challenges, and Chuck Forsyth showed me ways to improve my managerial quality in decision making.

Of all the leaders I've worked with, though, one stands out far and beyond the others: John P. Murphy, who was, by far, the best leader I have ever worked with. His intelligence, persistence in the face of challenge, and his insistence on staying focused on the business at hand were only a few of the attributes I admired then, and still do to this day. His business acumen was second to none, and he guided us through a huge merger, which I still believe should be a Harvard Business Review case study. I have great admiration for his leadership skills.

To these leaders, and more, I dedicate this book.

Dr. Jim Bohn
August, 2016

Table of Contents

FOREWORD

My leadership challenge in 2011 took the form of being asked to lead a large turnaround effort for a team of over 7000 people. They were seven years into a change initiative, and the change didn't stick. People were frustrated. They were angry. Results were lagging. Very early in this assignment, I reached out to Jim Bohn and asked him for counsel in driving the change. I asked him to review the change plan, sit in on the team meetings, and then provide input and feedback. The gift I received was advice rooted in experience, observation, and an eye for practicality.

"Don't damage the egos of the team members who invested so much of their effort in the previous initiative. They will be a big part of your future team." "Listen to the people who are invested in you. They want you to win and will keep you grounded." "Communicate to the frontline, and do it in their language, not ours."

As I read through this book and think back of the success of that turnaround, I can hear Jim's counsel echoing through. He achieves in this work what he has achieved throughout his career: he simplifies the complex into the actionable and practical. He speaks in real words, not corporate jargon. In doing so Jim creates a mechanism to share with scale and to help us all grow. Our role in this is to learn, apply, and repeat; and, after all is said and done (as Jim does here), pay it forward.

James Mylett, Senior Vice President - Service
Comfort Systems USA

FOREWORD

Jim is the Blue Collar Scholar. I have known him for over 20 years, as his career was in full throttle and leadership on fire; and now, watching his experience transform into a new vision is incredibly inspiring. Jim has been there for me as I have navigated my career choices; he has supported me and given specific, life changing advice. He gave me the hard truth to assist me in my growth and career trajectory.

This book will give very specific actions to take, not just theory. Leaders today like you, the reader, need specific things to say and do. Though mentally prepared, you need the nuts and bolts in various situations. We all do. You will find deep insights on how to gain from the struggles of leadership, including how to be resilient, how to make order out of chaos and, most importantly, where and how does humility affect your leadership. There are so many tidbits that pierce through the daily challenges of leading. Jim has a knack for turning these challenges into opportunities. Whether you're in a time of pure frustration or presented with a new opportunity, or just wondering how to take the next step, open the book and you will find new or renewed insights to help you move forward.

The ability to lead is something to be grateful for everyday; you are always growing and impacting others. Jim and his insights will help you find gratitude and guidance in this responsibility.

Elizabeth Thelen, Director of Entrepreneurship and Talent
The Water Council

INTRODUCTION

Leadership books are a cottage industry, filled with every imaginable framework of leadership, from Navy SEAL leadership to Home Shopping Channel leadership; to leading like Winnie-the-Pooh and Leadership for Dummies. Our book shelves are lined with these pamphlets, books and tomes. So, why another leadership book? The vantage point of this book: from the trenches to the boardroom.

Many leadership books come from either an academic focus or a military focus, or some other framework that, while interesting, may not be accessible in the corporate world. I lived the corporate world from all angles for four decades. I've seen brilliant and dynamic leaders, boring leaders, pathetic leaders, and outright brutal leaders, and I've had to work with them in all their warts and glory. I've also led award-winning teams in a complex Fortune 100 environment. The pages you'll read are principles I've used to get stuff done; these concepts work.

My approach to leadership is straightforward. Leaders are too busy to spend extensive time reading leadership books, and even less time to put leadership concepts into practice.

My book:

Is quick to read, but enduring in impact.

These chapters will take you a few minutes to read, but they provide enough thought-provoking insight to allow you to take the time to integrate the behavior into your leadership repertoire. Read a few pages; think about them; reflect on what they mean in your environment. Act.

Will help you get the job done.
As the Blue Collar Scholar, my goal is the same as my

father's: get the job done.

Does not separate leadership and management.

I believe the artificial division of leadership and management puts unnecessary strain on the person in "the chair." As leaders, we are both. We manage; we lead. It's a dance between vision and getting things done. If you're only about vision, you lose credibility; if you're only about the numbers, you lose the ability to inspire. We are both.

Gives you the right tools to get the right result.

The quick reads in this book are intended to be straightforward tools which can be applied *immediately*. If you're lost when working with your team, there are very specialized tools for improvement. Or, if you are flat out stuck in your leadership effectiveness, there are quick reads to address potential problems with patience, humor, and other attributes of leadership. If you're in an organizational quagmire, I have advice built from experience.

Yes, I have an earned doctorate. Yes, I've studied psychology, social science, and organizational theory in-depth—*but*—you will not find footnotes here, because you're extremely busy. Along the way, you'll see elements of Emotional Intelligence, Group Dynamics, Transformational Leadership Theory, Employee Engagement, Self-Determination Theory, Self-Efficacy, and Motivational Theory. You know it's there, but you want to get the job done. I've done my job so you can do yours.

The book is divided up into three major sections:

Self Leadership

Team Leadership

Organizational Leadership

Each section will give you the Tools, Techniques, and the Hot Spots to watch out for in each kind of leadership in quick, easy to read sections that will get you where you need to go.

Tools Practice these behaviors to directly influence an outcome. They are specific, direct, and have immediate application. Read and apply; repeat until it is a part of your leadership DNA!

Techniques These are more complex concepts requiring some thoughtful effort and reflection. Best to ponder these a bit and use them as a framework in your leadership role. Assess your situation in a coffee shop, then think about how to integrate these concepts into your work life/team.

Hot Spots These are situations, behaviors, and attitudes that can have negative influence on your team/organization. They generate a lot of heat (but not often light!). Reflecting carefully on them (and taking necessary, corrective action!) will change your style and situation.

Regardless of your challenges and what section you read, it is essential to keep in mind Bohn's Four Fundamental Principles of Human Behavior:

1. **If you push, people will shove.**
2. **People initiate and act on that which is important to them.**
3. **People need to know they made a difference.**
4. **Competence is deeply gratifying.**

These Principles have helped to guide my success in the business world, and they will serve you, as well, in your role as a Leader.

Let's get the job done.

Dr. Jim Bohn
August, 2016

SECTION I
SELF LEADERSHIP
Tools, Techniques & Hot Spots

TOOLS

Leadership Skill:
Bringing Order Out of Chaos

It's that moment you've been waiting for. They called your name. You're the one they're counting on to make this project/team/system/organization/work. You are the leader they've chosen. Your chance to make a reputation, an impact, a legend—it's now or never. *This is where leadership begins.*

The Reality
You're ready. You've been practicing, and you are *so* ready. Now it's show time. *And then the nightmare begins.* The project you expected has turned out to be a monster. The team you were asked to lead is a group of depressed employees. The system you've been asked to manage is a nightmare of IT spaghetti. Or, you've found out the organization you've been called to improve has a long track record of failures.

This is truly where leadership begins. Leadership is the ability to bring order out of chaos. In my opinion, that's what leadership ultimately means. But you may need a few tips.

Some fundamental steps for bringing order out of chaos:
The big goal here is to help people focus so they can renew their energy around a common set of goals. Get the facts, cut the non-essentials, and focus, focus, focus!

Although it sounds very impersonal, **finances come first.** What do you know about the budget? Is the group under water? Get those facts on the table as quickly as possible. No budget means working in the dark.

Who is on the team? What is their assessment of the situation? Listen carefully—who are the naysayers and what are their concerns? If legitimate, address them; if not, explain the need to get on board because the train is leaving the station.

What is the group doing? What strange projects are they working on? What unnecessary action is taking place right now? Where are people expending wasteful energy? Stop those things immediately—gently, but immediately.

Get rid of unnecessary activities. Stop running reports for about a week, and see who complains. (It's astonishing how we continue to run reports for someone who asked for a report *one time!*) What other arcane and peripheral projects are wasting employees energy? Cease them immediately!

Refocus the team on the essentials. "Here's what we need to accomplish," "Here's where we're expected to be in ten weeks," "This is our charter to achieve," "Here's where we fit into the organization."

Be graphic. Pictures help everyone to align. Build a simple, one-page map of where you're at and where you're going.

Repeat the process until you see daylight.

• Reward your team along the way ($50 worth of pizza goes a *long way).*

• Remain passionate about winning and let others know you plan to win. *Lead!*

• Help everywhere possible until the team is out of the storm.

Your Achievement

This great leadership skill of bringing order out of chaos is what separates real leaders from wannabes. This is difficult, demanding and—sometimes—fearsome work but, in my opinion and experience, it is the number one skill of great leaders, and the greatest means for leadership satisfaction.

Stand atop the mountain when the dragon has been slain my friends. You brought order out of chaos.

That's Leadership!

When people ask you what you do for a living, you can tell them: "I'm a leader—I bring order out of chaos."

Four Things You Gain from the Struggles of Leadership

You're in the middle of a mind-bending, dramatic challenge affecting hundreds, maybe thousands of people. Things are coming apart at the seams. The data isn't flowing through the system, people aren't being trained, customers are screaming, and upper management is not pleased. The sleepless nights are increasing, you're exhausted, and you're wondering if this pressure will ever end.

What value could this project possibly mean to you as a leader? It's likely it means everything.

Resilience **comes only through struggle.** While there are books, articles, movies, DVD's, and a myriad of other tools available to learn *about* resilience, the fact is, resilience comes only from persisting in the face of struggle. Resilience is that amazing, yet invisible, essence that drives motivation to succeed in the face of defeat. It is a wondrous psychological gift you give to yourself through the pain.

Leader Efficacy **is the result of facing and managing through the struggle.** The sense of "I can do this," also known as self-efficacy, comes only through the struggle. Easy assignments and projects will never fill a reservoir of deep efficacy, but facing the challenges of projects that are out of control, people issues that are seemingly endless, and overcoming unforeseen circumstances with a deft sense of control only come through the struggle—there is no other way.

Leader Credibility **is the result of facing and managing through the struggle.** When people think of you, do they say "just another manager" or do they secretly, grudgingly stand in awe of your achievements? When you've been through the fire, and you have persisted and completed the most difficult of tasks, people will respect your capabilities, but you can't get there unless you go through the swamp, the mosquitoes, and the heat and humidity of frustrations that we call the organizational workplace.

Self-Respect is the reward of facing and managing through the struggle. At the end of the day, every leader wants to know that they made a difference. There's that moment of achievement when the team rises together and shouts: "We did this!" As the leader who stayed the course; as the leader who would not give up; as the leader who took on the toughest of the tough projects, there is absolute joy in raising a glass and smiling to oneself, whilst basking in the glow of achievement. It's only through the struggle that we obtain these things—there is no way around it. Persist, all the way to the top!

The One Question Leaders Should Ask Themselves Every Day

You want to influence your organization for all the right reasons. You've made a significant investment in your education, and you want to share your competence. You have deep experience in multiple disciplines, and you want to help your organization succeed. You're confident that your ideas will be effective. Your ability to bring teams together is second to none, and you want to demonstrate your capabilities. At a personal level, you want to advance your career path.

Here's the tough news: You're competing with every other leader for organizational resources.

As a leader, you compete with scores of other organizational members for resources: for help, for funding and, especially, for executive attention. How do you gain what other leaders (*legitimately*) want? Resources, even in the most powerful organizations, are still limited.

As a leader, you need to influence many who do not report to you. Other leaders in your organization also influence those who do not report to them. The challenges all leaders face are very common. So, what makes one leader stand out among the others? What makes one leader more influential and effective than another? What is the ultimate deciding factor in your organizational influence?

Ask yourself this one question every day. I believe the answer to this question will tell you how effective you'll be in the workplace. **"Do people find it easy to work with me?"**

Do people walk the other way when they see you in the hall, or are they glad to see you? Do people extend their visits with you during conversation, or are they checking their watch and saying, "I have a meeting to attend?" If so, it may be that you're making it hard for others to work with you. Something in your work behavior causes undue stress for others—*and that's not a good thing.* What does "easy to work with" look like in practice? Like this:

- You answer questions clearly and succinctly, so people know where they stand.
- You keep commitments.
- You display competence when sharing information.
- You respond quickly to requests.
- You're cooperative and willing to help.
- You take on your share of the work.
- Your yes is yes, and your no is no.
- You don't play games with people's time—people know when you're negotiating for time, funding, and *quid pro quo.*
- You have a "Let's get to work" attitude.
- Most importantly, people don't need to expend significant emotional energy when they work with you.

"Easy to work with" does not mean agreeing to everything. Easy to work with doesn't mean we need to make people feel all fluffy when they work with us, or that you need to be a pushover for every decision or request. It means this: do people feel like they're respected when they're in your presence? Do they feel like they matter when you ask for their help? If so, you're easy to work with, and that is one of the most powerful means of influence in the world.

I am merely refining what I learned long ago: In Robert Cialdini's brilliant work, *Influence,* he spends a significant time on "Liking;" the idea that people will work with those whom they like. People in the workplace like people who are easy to work with. Are you that person?

The Importance of Base Camp

People who climb Mount Everest talk of establishing a "base camp;" a place of safety and certainty in preparation for the ascent. I have not participated in that amazing achievement, but I picked up the phrase a long time ago, and have used the analogy in my career to sustain me through some rather tough "climbs" along the way. It's essential that leaders maintain a base camp throughout their careers; to sustain sanity, to protect themselves from stress, and to prepare for, and recover from, stressful events. After all, our careers are a "climb," are they not? Here's what a base camp provides to leaders and climbers, alike:

A place of Safety At base camp, climbers know they are not in danger, but they are preparing for something dangerous.

A place of Preparation The climb requires careful thinking, thoughtful planning for food supplies, anticipation of emergencies, and deliberate ways to communicate once the climb is underway.

A place of Rest At base camp, climbers can be at ease; relax and allow their minds and bodies to gain strength for the road ahead.

A place of Replenishment Base camp represents a climb in itself, because it takes several weeks—sometimes months—to get to the bottom of the mountain. Supplies can be replenished as the leader prepares for what is ahead.

A place to Regroup Sometimes attempts to ascend are met with hostile weather or other unforeseen circumstances. Base camp provides a place to regain strategy, to reorganize and to rethink the approach to the climb.

A place to Recover Sometimes people get injured on the climb, but they are unable to completely descend to a valley for several days due to weather conditions.

Here's what base camp means to career climbers:

A place of Safety One's home is a place of safety during a career climb. It is a place without danger; a place where one can plan without risk.

A place of Preparation Base camp is the quiet place to consider the approach up the mountain; the necessary actions which must be taken to achieve the summit.

A place of Rest Again, one's home is a place to be at ease; to relax and allow minds and bodies to regain strength. Shutting off the computer and cell phone for a while is a mandatory part of career base camp.

A place of Replenishment Good camaraderie and strong teamwork create an environment for replenishment. Sometimes one member of the team feels stronger than others and, on other days, a different team member may feel stronger. Great team members are a "social base camp" you can turn to when things are tough, to get through hard times.

A place to Regroup Some strategies don't work very well when we're working on a major project. Base camp is a place where we take the time to remove all the distractions of survival, so we can rethink and change our approach.

A place to Recover Sometimes, we fail in our career strategies, and sometimes we fall off a cliff. Base camp is the place to recover. *A sacred place that belongs to you!*

It could be your local library or a forest. For some, the water or a 20 mile bike ride to decompress. For others, it could be rock climbing, or collecting stamps, or a cool drink on a extraordinary day. Whatever you do in your career, for all the reasons I have listed, protect your base camp. It is a necessary part of a successful career.

Managing Your Time Means Managing Yourself

The very idea of time management is an odd thing, don't you think? The very idea that we *manage* time is almost silly. The clock is what the clock is. Immutable time. 24 hours a day, ad infinitum. The truth is this: we don't manage time, *we manage ourselves*—or not.

People exhibit odd behavior in their desperate attempts to manage time. I've seen people rush at the last minute, trying to rescue a situation they could have resolved months ago. I've seen students drink Red Bull so they can knock out a 50 page paper the night before it is due, and tell me they like the pressure (even though they're freaking out!). They could have done parts of the paper over time and saved themselves all kinds of pain, including poor grades!

The discipline of self-management is the key to ultimate productivity.

In our work lives, time is...well ... money! Yet we are often our own worst enemies with this finite substance. It is not time we must manage, it is ourselves. So! I've developed a short list of thoughts for a bit of self-reflection (when you have time ...).

Time is wasted through:

Self-imposed restraining orders, such as perfectionism (overdoing things of little importance), an inability to move quickly from one subject to another (slow uptake from one situation to another), procrastination, and indecision (generally based in fear). These are all self-imposed behaviors that cost time. Through practice and self-discipline, they can be overcome.

System overload Problems An inability to focus because you have too much going on due to a lack of prioritization, as well as a lack of effective delegation.

He said/She said Complex Like blaming others for failure, making excuses for an inability to plan and prepare, and using Myers-Briggs stereotypes as a fall back plan for failure. *("I'm an ENFP!")* Excuses are expensive time drains.

Nice guys finish last Syndrome In other words, the inability to say "no" (and stick to it), and allowing too many interruptions (which we also own) causes great losses of time. Why does every small child get away with "no?" They don't change their minds—why do we?

Low battery Problem Wearing out yourself (and others!) by giving people the "Atlantic Monthly" version of an issue, when you could have used the "Reader's Digest" version. You not only tire yourself, you wear out your welcome with key people who will dread seeing you in the hallway when you want to ask for help. Save words, save time. Not everything needs explaining. Move on.

Memory losses due to delaying or ineffectively recording the ideas, minutes, notes, and critical pieces of information you will need later on. In manufacturing, this is rework; in white collar roles, it is also rework, but in the form of searching for things you need but can't find, or having to remind people of agreements that were never formalized. Backtracking is expensive; discipline of good record keeping saves precious energy.

Mr. Miyagi Issue "First learn balance." Managers must learn to avoid spending too much time on a good thing; in short, focusing on the things they like (*prioritization by pleasure*). Without balance in our thinking, we waste time.

What you notice from these observations is that the emotional impact of these disciplines cost us more than the actual work we do. We do not manage time, we manage ourselves—or not. The discipline of self-management is the key to ultimate productivity. Controlling our anxiety through these disciplines allow us to take full advantage of the 24 hours we have every day.

Principle #1—You cannot manage time, but if you're not careful, it will manage you.

- Determine for yourself the difference between indecision and intentional waiting.
- The easy way becomes the hard way. Too much time spent in the easy causes a whole lot of troublesome work down the road.

Principle #2—You can manage yourself; no one else is going to do that.

- Commit to a task and complete it; self explanatory.
- Purpose guides the mind. If you know what you want to accomplish, you can rule out a whole lot of other stuff. Focus, goal setting, and determination are the elements of success.
- Build a base camp. Base camp is the critical, predictable

component of our life which allows us to branch out and do other things. We are responsible for the disciplines and actions that help us get things done.

- Physical condition contributes to the effectiveness of managing ourselves; do you exercise?
- Mental concentration; manage the fleeting thoughts!
- Focus your learning around your greatest weakness.

Principle #3—You can influence situations to more effectively get things done. Remember Bohn's second law of Human Motivation: *People initiate and act on that which is important to them.* People are often the reason for impeded progress—but why? With the exceptions of accidents and most illnesses, we own the interruptions in our lives. Here are some questions to ask yourself:

- Who are we asking for help? Have we carefully considered whether a person can truly help us?
- How are we asking for help? We know where we want to go, what we want to do, and what we need to accomplish, but does anyone else? How are we organizing the thinking of others so they can help us?
- When are we asking for help, and how often? We own how others can help us. Others are bombarded with requests and data—how do we get our requests to the top of those priorities?
- Remember that people forget. Organizational amnesia occurs every day. Your memory must exceed the memory of the organization.
- *We* own the communication process. *We* own the thoroughness, speed, and quality of how we come across. How can you be helpful to the person helping you? How do you prepare people to help you be successful? Do you take time

to help them understand?

Principle #4—Spend time to buy time. On aircraft. On quiet mornings. (*In boring meetings!*) Whenever you have the time, ponder the time ahead. Build out schedules on simple pieces of paper to map out what's down the road. Think about what is necessary in your own development to improve your self-management.

Its time.

The High Calling of Developing Others

In moments of honest, private reflection, all of us struggle with the lifetime value of our work. Why do we do what we do? Does it matter? As a leader, I have found deep personal satisfaction from truly developing people and watching them succeed. *Developing people is a calling.* With a four decade perspective of leadership, and using servant leadership as a philosophical framework, I found that developing people had an immense impact on others and also on my own leadership satisfaction. I believe leaders will find value as they take time to reflect on the incredible importance of the calling to develop others. A few perspectives:

Take the long view. Developing people is hard work. It takes time away from other projects, emails, conference calls, and the nonstop, day-to-day pressures of managing. Developing people requires thoughtful effort, consideration of each individual, and follow-through to ensure action takes place.

Developing others is its own reward. I had a team member who found it difficult to speak to large groups. It caused him some serious career challenges, and he became more and more anxious about addressing customers. Other leaders who he worked for simply pushed him to speak, and he failed. Under my leadership, we developed a plan to get him some training in public speaking. It took time, persuasion, funding, and a few days of his time away from the job, but it was essential.

Taking the long view means people don't grow overnight. If we view them with a frustrated sense of "Why can't you get this done?" we are not developing them, we are using them.

Understand your philosophical foundation for developing others. Have you considered *why* you do what you do? Clearly your skill-set (finance, legal, accounting, operations, engineering, and human resources) is a valuable tool in your management toolbox, but how do you answer your own "why?" Is there a part of your mindful workspace that says, *I intentionally develop other people; I create paths for their success; I anticipate what they need; I find satisfaction in the achievements of others?*

Reflect on the satisfaction gained in developing others. *Developing others is its own reward.* Looking back over my career, I see people who have moved up, whose lives were bettered, who improved skills and gained motivational insights from the work I did. There is deep satisfaction knowing you helped someone else achieve great things.

Questions for assessing your skills in developing others:

- Have you given thought to how you go about developing others?

- What are your core leadership motivations?

- What do you believe are the values of developing people?

- What successes have you seen over time when you applied effort to people development?

- What is the value to organizations?

We talk so often about the need to retain the best people and developing a more focused leadership team. People will stick with leaders who have demonstrated that they are interested in the long term development of their staff. People know when you sense that they are more than a job; they know when you show that their development is a calling.

The Joy of Leadership:
Why We Do What We Do

I had a deeply challenging team member. I was at the verge of wanting to terminate the individual. I thought, *I'm going to give this one last try.* So, we had a conversation. It was intense, direct, and clear. I offered my assistance if the person was willing to work with me, *and* the option to leave if they chose not to make an effort. Nearly a year later, the individual offered this: "Your feedback has not only changed my work, but my marriage and family life, as well." That moment was deeply satisfying. My leadership had an impact.

Employee Engagement is not personally satisfying to most leaders. Since the advent of Employee Engagement research, we hear a lot about Employee Satisfaction. *(In my opinion, employee engagement surveys are so commonplace, they've nearly lost their impact)*

With so much focus on Employee Satisfaction, we've lost sight of a significant factor in organizational effectiveness: ***Leader Satisfaction.*** Without satisfied leaders, employee engagement scores are likely to remain the same as they have for over a decade. Leaders are chronically (and appropriately) held accountable for project success, for achievement of strategic plans, for employee development, for annual budgets, for disciplinary actions, for completion of corporate compliance, and for the day-to-day actions of reporting and execution, but we'd all agree there's more to life than merely accomplishing tasks. *There must be something more.* A life's work as a leader must carry with it a much deeper meaning and impact.

Leaders can assess their own satisfaction with their work by taking the time to reflect on two elements of their personal impact: Developing people and developing teams.

What are the elements of work life that give leaders a sense of purpose and value?

- Leader satisfaction in developing people.
- The word "development" is so overused that it, too, may have lost some of its meaning in the past few years, yet the concept is still accurate. Leaders do develop people. The problem is, we've never truly defined how leaders gain satisfaction from employee development.
- Assessing the skills people have, and taking those skills to the next level, along with assigning developmental tasks that will improve the competence of our people, are part of developing people. Overall, our satisfaction as leaders depends on our efforts in inspiring others to levels of personal achievement they never dreamed were possible!

Here are a few statements to reflect upon to assess your satisfaction as a leader of people:

- I *know* my influence has improved the competence of the individuals I have led.
- I sense a great deal of pride when one of the people I've hired goes on to greater things than I have achieved.
- The model of leadership I have demonstrated has changed the lives of others.

Leadership satisfaction in developing Teams So much of our time as leaders comes down to building the right team. Did we get the right people on board? Did we structure things effectively? Did we allow for "voice" without over-whelming the project with too much data? Did we remove people who were not effective? Did we provide the support people needed to achieve the end goal? Did we reward people fairly and without favoritism? Did we win?

If we can answer "yes" to the majority of those questions, we've done our job. We've done what was *expected*. But, achieving the *necessary* is not enough to achieve a sense of leader satisfaction.

Here are a few statements to reflect upon to assess your satisfaction as a leader of teams:

- I know my expertise at coordinating people made a major difference in accomplishing the goal.
- My relationships with other managers and leaders has a dramatic impact on the success of my team.
- The people I work with would work with me any day of the week, because they know I care about their competence, welfare, and achievement.

We spend a third of our lifetimes at work. As leaders, we need to gain a sense of our own satisfaction with our role. In addition, organizations need to refocus training and development on (1) the meaning of leadership in the lives of those who lead, (2) the meaning of leadership influence on those they lead, and (3) the meaning of leadership influence on the corporations they serve.

Are you satisfied with your leadership? If not, what needs to change?

What Leadership Persona
do you Convey?

To truly lead is to influence. Leadership influence is the result of many things. Ultimately, leadership effectiveness is the psychological impact of a person engaged in relationships with others. Leadership influence is, in short, *persona*, a word critical for understanding leadership influence. *Leadership Persona is the composite psychological impact of multiple personal characteristics, including image persona and behavior persona.* It is the person we convey to those we work with every day. It is a barometer of our influence.

Image Persona When I speak of *image persona*, I'm talking about the persona a person is projecting through their material choices and mannerisms, such as the clothing they wear, the way they walk, or even the way their office is decorated (which hopefully does, but may not, reflect the person that they really are).

Image persona matters. For example, I think we'd all agree Steve Jobs' classic turtleneck look conveyed a persona. "I'm here to work; here as an artist; here to create something." And he did. Clothing communicates persona. It's the first thing people notice about us before we even speak. We convey an image through what we wear, and that image is influential. Walking into work like we just rolled out of bed conveys a persona, and it impacts our influence. People won't say it, but they know it.

The way we walk conveys an image. I recall one of my first bosses telling me, "The way you walk down a hall demonstrates you're going somewhere; you have intention to get things done." I was very young, but I never forgot those words. Deportment, in general, is an element of leadership persona. *Persona is influence.*

Behavior Persona We've talked of image persona. Now let's talk about behavior; how we act in the context of others.

- **Punctuality** The use of time is a powerful element of leader persona. Whether we are late or early, or exactly on time, we communicate several things. We communicate our own level of self-importance (our time) or our concerns about the importance of others (their time). We model precisely how we expect others to manage time when they are with us. We communicate urgency, expediency, focus, efficiency, clarity, effectiveness, and competence through our use of time. Our time behavior is a large element of leadership persona.
- **Presence** The sense people have of our true level of engagement with them is our level of presence. People know if we are "with them" during a discussion—especially during this day of screens and devices. There's a reason we use the phrase "paying attention." Attention is expensive. It is costly. It is an investment. It is a major element of leadership persona and influence. It is eye contact. It is attentive listening. For people know whether we are with them or somewhere else.
- **Persistence** I recall an employee walking by my office one time when I was hanging my head down after a rough meeting. She said, "It's not a good idea for others to see you so beat up and disheartened, even if you are." How we persist in the face of obstacles immensely conveys who we

are. It is an element of leadership persona that we may not be aware of, but others are. Do people believe we will get the job done? Are we persistent in the face of pressures, demands, confusing uncertainties and unforeseen events? In short, are we unshakable?

- **Patience** Leadership patience may sound like an odd concept—after all, the world is moving quickly! Who has time for patience with staff, with teams, and with the development of a new product or solution? We need to get the job done! And yet, a few moments of leadership patience have a psychological impact that goes well beyond any motivational speeches or corporate incentives. Leadership patience is a major element in leadership persona.

- **Precision** Great leaders know the facts *cold*. They are accurate in their thinking, in their assessments of the capabilities of others, and in their ability to "size up" a situation. They are skilled at finding the right words for the right time. In short, they are careful and diplomatic in their communication.

The composite of these elements (and several more, including leadership wisdom and leadership humor) dictate your organizational effectiveness as a leader. These are the elements of leadership influence, the elements of the persona you project every day. Pay close attention to what you convey.

The Invisible Elements of Leadership Persona

We have all heard the phrase, "Your reputation precedes you." Reputation is that invisible element of persona that enters a room long before we do. Reputation takes a variety of forms.

- **Reputation for causing fear in the hearts of followers** This special reputation belongs to those who are cruel leaders, with a penchant for unpredictable and dangerous behavior, including intentionally embarrassing people in front of their peers (and even prone to physical assaults). Think Captain Ahab.

- **Reputation for Helpfulness** This individual is known for their capability to offer assistance or recommendations for where assistance might be attained. This person has a genuine interest in the success of others, and they are more than words— they get things done.

- **Reputation for Creativity** This individual is known for unexpected insights and odd, yet effective, options. They may be quirky, and even unconventional, but they have the ability to see unusual aspects of a problem.

- **Reputation for Solutions** This person is known as a pragmatic individual who has successfully resolved complex and difficult situations many times.

- **Reputation for Trustworthiness (or the absence of it)** More powerful than the words "I love you" are the words "I trust you." When people place their trust in someone, they are surrendering their own control, and acknowledging someone else has now taken over their time, their energy, and their skills. It takes risk to trust. People know the invisible truth: *Does this person keep their word? Do they make public commitments in the presence of their peers and superiors?* Some have an invisible persona that can only be described as double dealing. These are the political people who will win at all costs.

- **Reputation for Managerial Courage (or lack of it)** Do they risk their own success by taking on massive, extraordinary and overtly complex projects—and often succeed? Few want to take risks, but a person who displays managerial courage is known by their willingness to raise their hand when others back away. Do they take a stand for those *not* in the room? When people are berated or unfairly criticized, a person with managerial courage will be known as a justice seeker, a truth teller, and someone who refuses to listen to mythology (organizational gossip) about another individual.

- **Reputation for Integrity** Do they demonstrate integrity at all costs? Do they understand the cost of their decisions, but maintain principles without regard for the risk of their own job? These people are revered by others as someone who will never alter their statements for personal gain.

- **Reputation for Credibility** Are they known to get the job done? Do they have a track record of achievements? Do they make commitments that are achievable? Or, are they filled with excessive words, PowerPoint presentations, and clichés, yet without true achievements?

Making the Persona *Personal* In different ways and at different levels of strength, these elements comprise our invisible persona; that persona you and I project well in advance of our entry into a room. It is the person we are in the minds of others. It is worth taking the time to reflect on the persona we are projecting, and even more important to find ways to correct and improve the ways we are perceived—*the effectiveness of our leadership depends on it.* Before you enter a room, the invisible elements of your persona are already there.

Fuel Your Leadership Motivation by Managing Your Nine Lives

To merely survive in business is not a pleasant thing. None of us wants to simply "check the box" at 5:00 p.m., just grateful to have made it one more day. Let's face it: that's a tough way to live (and it's true, we've all done it for a section of our careers). Yet leaders have access to nine kinds of motivation which can enhance any organizational or personal situation. Overlook any of these and you may miss one of the greatest contributors to your overall well-being and success. The nine lives allow us to live life in all its richness, even in the midst of struggle and hardship.

Foundational motivations At the base we find the basics! If we do not manage our *physical* life, the other lives suffer greatly. Through some means, we must manage our physical lives. While we don't all need to be Olympic athletes (few are!), our physical nature requires care as the foundation to our other lives. Neglect of our physical life has long range implications.

Our *social* life includes friends, families, spouses, co-workers and other people who influence us every day. Research shows the critical importance of effective and rich relationships.

Our *emotional* life consists of managing negative feelings and balancing them with a positive outlook. Whole books and research have been written on this area of managerial impact (the literature on emotional intelligence is a great place to begin understanding this life).

Mid-level motivation Our *cognitive* life is where we fill the motivational fuel tank. It is the place we breathe with our minds; where the air of interesting ideas and concepts flow and cause us to step outside, then inside, ourselves. Reading, thinking, learning, considering, discussing, contemplating, writing, debating, listening, and learning are deep motivational resources to our lives.

Our **adventure** life causes us to get stronger in one very specific area: confidence. Without the occasional adventure, we are not balanced. We get bored, tired, and unenthusiastic about living. We need to stretch, risk, *even feel fear,* to get back into balance. Then we can enjoy the accomplishments of the risk. Adventure life also teaches us volition.

Our **vocational** life is the place that earns us bread, butter and the occasional glass of beer.

Higher Order Motivation   The highest level of our lives are those places where we reach well beyond ourselves into places of exceptional achievement.

Our **artistic** lives require careful cultivation. Although the skill of the art may be genetic or talent, the effort required for us to grow the artistic life takes many years. Witness those people in your life who are very good at the artistic side and you find them seeing things differently. I believe everyone has an artistic life; while some are more gifted in performance, all have the ability for deep levels of appreciating beauty, whether it is a perfectly thrown pass or a Renoir. Music, drama, dance, poetry, and art comprise this life.

Service life consists in those things that require sacrifice on our part for the benefit of others. This typically takes form in a voluntary, altruistic activity.

Ultimately, our **spiritual** lives take us to another place; another dimension; another realm. What's included here? Spiritual life is a sense of something far greater than oneself. For those who do not believe in spiritual things, this life may the life of the highest ethical standards or the influence of what the Greeks saw as the Good, the True and the Beautiful. Applying energy to our spiritual lives allows us to rise above the many difficulties of life by seeing things in terms of the eternal, the heroic, and the enduring.

And, as you've discovered, they fit together. In the workplace, in our families, in our volunteer activities, and in our leisure, they are all intertwined. *Mastery of one life gives us the power to manage the others: Volition.*

Ultimately, I have observed that all of life is about a 10th life— our volitional life. By choosing, we build our futures. Our choices create our options. Our choices create our next step. In my opinion, learning to manage our volitional lives is the key to managing everything else. *Our volitional life is the very heart of our motivational resources. It can be something as simple as managing tedium by accessing these other lives, or demonstrating persistence in a complex, demanding and difficult situation.*

You have (at least) ten ways to fuel your leadership motivation. Determining your strengths and weaknesses will provide you with a path for increased leadership effectiveness. Today is the day; now is the time.

(With a tip of the hat to Abraham Maslow).

Valuing Your Value as a Leader

Oh no! Dr. Bohn is going to take us on a voyage across the Sea of Self-Esteem; or, a hair commercial that says "you're worth it" (and, as you can tell from my picture, that marketing has little influence on me these days). Nope—not going there, my friends! In truth, no self-respecting leader wants to take that trip. Leaders don't see themselves as needy, unfulfilled people floating in self-doubt. They're leaders!

But, we all may need to take a step back and look at the value we bring to our organizations. From my vantage point, I see six ways leaders should value their value:

Your Experience Whether you've been a leader for six months or thirty years, your experience has value. Whatever you've been through in life has created a framework for seeing the world. You're alert to dangerous situations because you've "been there; done that." You've also experienced situations outside the workplace—volunteering, in sports teams, in educational settings, and in non-profit organizations. That means you've worked with people, and working with people is the heart of leadership.

Your Counsel When other managers come to you asking for advice or input or insight, your counsel has value. In the very act of advising others, you are limiting some of their distractions and helping them focus on their goals. Through the questions you ask, through your body language, and through your warnings and encouragement, your counsel helps others achieve things with less heartache and headache.

Your Judgment Judgment (the older sister of opinion) is built on your experience, your education, your track record, your failures, and your exceptional achievements. Judgment is a thing of beauty. When you state something in very clear terms, such as, "In my judgment, this isn't going to work because ...," you've opened a door to dialogue by putting a stake in the ground—a point to argue from. Even if people continue to go in a different direction after you've made your point, know that you helped them assess and assize a situation, simply by communicating the strong convictions that arise from judgment.

Your Influence Influence is a strange, ghostlike power that some leaders bring into a room by their sheer presence. For some of you, influence is so powerful people can sense it in your speech. The legends of your accomplishments precede you, and people know who you are, even though you've never met them. Influence comes from persona, charm, conviction, experience, brilliant communications, careful negotiation, and a willingness to hear other points of view; and, sometimes, your greatest influence is those awful projects no one else took on for fear of failure—but you did, and you achieved the impossible.

The power of your network The people you can contact within your organization are worth thousands, even millions of dollars. Think of it this way: you've developed relationships with people through time; you know what they can do. You know their strengths, weaknesses, and THEIR networks. You know when to engage them, and when to only ask for advice. That's valuable stuff, readers, because your network is like a superhighway that accelerates decision-making, enabling rapid progress and change.

I recently spoke with a person who just started at a company. He knows the uphill battle to gain a powerful network, but he also knows the value. And so he will continue to work at increasing the power of his network.

Your ability to get things done Beyond the five values listed above (and largely because of them), you have value in your ability to get stuff done. After all the PowerPoint slides and presentations are long forgotten, your reputation to get things done is your supreme value.

Your value is powerful. Build it. Take pride in it. Enjoy it. Don't rest on it. Grow it.

SECTION I
SELF LEADERSHIP
Tools, Techniques & Hot Spots

TECHNIQUES

Leadership Humility:
What It Is, and What It Isn't

There is much talk these days of the value of leadership humility. I am convinced the topic is valuable, and not faddish, but being raised for several reasons:

- Social media can easily display a leader's failures within nanoseconds. Leadership failure has become more prominent because of social media.
- Gen-X and Millennials are all about "transparency," which is code for, "I can't trust you unless I really know who you are." While we Baby Boomers all believed that notion, the recent generations are pressing the issue very hard.
- Did I mention social media?

Let's start with what leadership humility is *not*:
- Leadership humility is not a complete acceptance of any and all ideas at any moment in time.
- Leadership humility does not wear a pushover persona which is easily influenced in a hundred directions.
- Leadership humility is not a constant, feigned berating of one's own skills in the face of others.

Here's what I believe constitutes leadership humility:
- Leadership humility is the confident exertion of one's power, without damaging the dignity of others.
- Leadership humility is the ability to listen to all parties, without imposing an image of elevated separation (In other words, leaders are not "above all that.").
- Leadership humility is the ability to admit mistakes and

learn from them in an organizational context.

- Leadership humility is the willingness to share the victory, and the acknowledgement that it takes many to win.
- Leadership humility is the respect for all those who have built the path before us; making the way through their sacrifice and prescience.
- Leadership humility never abdicates responsibility.

You may have other beliefs about what constitutes leadership humility. One thing we know for sure: leadership arrogance is not welcome by anyone in *any* generation.

The Priceless Value of Leadership Humor

When I am asked about qualities I value in a leader, people are often surprised to hear me say, "A leader needs a great sense of humor."

Why would a sense of humor be a key trait in a good leader?

- People are under radical stress in the workplace.
- People work incredibly long hours.
- People give their lives in support of a job.
- People lose precious family time in support of the work-place.
- People's lives *outside the workplace* are often complicated, adding to the stress (Work-Life Balance, anyone?).

Objections to leadership humor:
Humor can be perceived as disrespect, lewdness, and crass behavior, sometimes even leading to harassment charges. Humor diminishes the seriousness and gravity of the work. Leaders need to be dour, grim, and stern; "Stiff upper lip," and all that sort of thing. Humor demeans a leader and turns him or her into a class clown, causing a loss of respect from employees. Humor can be misperceived in a global environment.

Let's take a closer look at each objection in turn:
Lewd behavior and humor has *no place* at work (or anywhere else, but that's my personal bias in favor of respect for others). Clearly, any humor that harms another individual or causes someone to be uncomfortable is out of place, but that's not the kind of humor I'm talking about. I'm talking about having a bit of fun in the midst of stress.

When the situation requires gravity, the leader knows it and the people know it. They all sense the need for seriousness, but a constant pressure of seriousness creates emotional distress for employees, adding even *more* stress to their work. People need to laugh now and then; "comic relief" is valuable in the workplace.

If a leader is *constantly* cutting up, he or she will lose the respect of the people, but an intelligent quip at the right time not only adds to a leader's persona, it makes him or her *human!* With the exception of warfare, I can't imagine a place where the occasional quip is out of place or, better yet, self-deprecating humor—harms no one, but does the job. A leader who can tell a joke (and, even better, *take* a joke!) will create an emotional bond that is hard to break under pressure.

In a global environment, things don't often translate well but, if you explain a joke or concept, people across the world love to laugh! One of my greatest communication victories ever was to tell a joke cross culturally with a group of Japanese business people, who laughed very heartily at a punch line...after it was explained through an interpreter.

Leadership humor is free, but also priceless.
Effective humor endears people to a leader, because laughter is good for the soul. It eases pain, refreshes, and adds energy when needed. Never underestimate the motivational power of leadership humor; it demonstrates a quick mind, intelligence, emotional sensitivity and, most of all, develops a bond of human contact unattainable by any other means. A little laughter goes a long way.

Leadership Communication is Physics:
Energy, Friction, Inertia, and Momentum

Communication is one of those odd words that drives executives crazy. Maybe we should explain it differently, analogous to physics. Good communication creates energy. Poor communication creates friction, inertia, and loss of momentum.

Good communication generates energy. The motivation of your people is the single most precious resource in your company. Employee motivation is the energy source powering organizational success. Why would you waste it? Effective communication generates energy among team members.

Poor communication builds employee friction. Precious organizational energy is lost when poor communication creates friction and employee inertia. *Friction occurs when two objects are occupying the same space.* That applies to employee relationships, too! Ineffective communication causes friction because people fear for their jobs. They hear rumors and gossip, and they assume things that are not true. *Ineffective communication causes friction when people don't know their role or responsibility.* They become frustrated with one another and, thus, point fingers, lay blame, and argue. This creates friction, which generates a lot of heat, but not much light!

Poor communication builds employee inertia. Employee Inertia occurs when they're not sure what to do, such as with:

- **Obtuse Visioning** When people don't know where the organization is going, they sit and wait. That's inertia.

- **Ineffective Direction Setting** When people are unsure what they're supposed to do, they wait. That's inertia.

- **Incomplete Decision Making** When people have only part of the information they need, they wait. That's inertia.

- **Miscoordinated Action** When people hear three different versions of what they're supposed to do, they wait. That's called inertia.

- **Incomplete Follow-Through** Leaders drop the ball! People get reassigned—without a successor! So people wait some more, because they're unsure what to do. That's called inertia.

The Effects of Employee Inertia: Ineffective communication stifles energy and leads to low productivity, leading to more time spent on people struggles than output. Ineffective communication ultimately leads to uncertainty, and then fear of failure, fear of incompetence, fear of making a mistake—often leading to costly rework! Ineffective communication causes the loss of precious organizational energy.

How can you reduce Employee Inertia? Your communications provide a context for decision making, allowing people to answer this question: "What do I need to do to support the organization?" Your communication provides a context for prioritization: "What do I need to do to do first?"

The danger if this isn't done? People become paralyzed and ineffective. The reason it isn't done: because leaders, themselves, are unsure of where they're going!

As a leader, you need to know where you're going and to develop effective ways for prioritizing projects. Take the time to clearly state expectations, direction, and the end goal.

Managerial concern for ego intensifies inertia in these ways:

- **Imperfection** Managers fear loss of credibility if they communicate something that could change. *Get over it.*

- **Image**   Managers may have concern about not having all the answers. *Get over it.*

- **Insulation**   Managers are afraid to give up power, hence the arcane phrase, "need to know." *Get over it.*

Good communication builds acceleration. *Acceleration happens when a path is clear and safe.* Provide people a knowledge of the future. ("People expect leaders in this business to know where they're going.") Provide knowledge of roles ("Who's on first?"). Provide knowledge that people are supported in their actions.

Good communication builds momentum. *Momentum happens when one good project leads to another—and another, and another.* Two specific actions you can take to increase momentum:
1. *Provide knowledge of what has happened,* so people can feel a sense of efficacy, achievement, movement, and momentum.
2. *Provide knowledge of victories,* to allow the emotional sense of achievement, and to build power and energy for the next project.

Good communication generates organizational efficiency. *Efficiency happens when the amount of output is greater than the input.* Getting people to work together takes effort, clear focus, and focused agendas. That's called leadership. Good leaders reduce friction and inertia, and increase acceleration and momentum through great communication. That's what organizations want and what customers expect!

The Power of
Leadership Patience

Organizational pressures compel us to act. Leaders are under immense organizational pressures: the pressure to achieve more revenue and profit than last year; the pressure to complete projects ahead of time, with less cost; the pressure to introduce more products at a faster rate; the pressure to respond more quickly to customer requests; the pressure to meet corporate objectives for employee engagement scores; the pressure to achieve higher levels of customer satisfaction; the pressure to produce five nines of up-time; the pressure to meet government requirements; the pressure to expand into new markets in new geographic territories; and, the pressure to achieve these things ethically, under the scrutiny of the public eye. ***This is reality for today's leaders. And you want me to be ... patient!?***

Leader impatience creates an unwelcome environment for followers. Many who read this have been the object of leadership impatience. It is an unpleasant and unwelcome emotional experience. We've also been impatient with our own followers, and we've seen their reactions.

Know this: leadership patience *does not equal procrastination.* The critics of leadership patience will be quick to say, "This looks like indecisiveness or, even worse, it looks like fear. We're leaders—we act." To them, leadership looks like this:

"Get the &#%@@$& job done!"
But leader patience does not equal procrastination. Procrastination is indecisiveness. Patience is a more complex and pow-

erful leadership attribute. Procrastination drags out decisions; patience leads to more effective decisions. Procrastination makes team members crazy; patience builds their confidence.

Leadership patience builds confidence in followers. For the past two decades, Daniel Goleman has taught us about the critical impact of leadership emotions in the workplace. We *know* both intuitively and objectively that impatience builds mistrust, fear, anger, resentment, and frustration with our team members. The reverse is also true. Followers who recognize the immensity of the pressures you face as a leader also acknowledge the price of patience. Leaders find ways to reduce anxiety so people can make effective decisions using their cerebral cortex, instead of the deep emotional centers of the brain.

Leadership patience is the ability to carefully value the personal interactions required to accomplish a goal.

- **Listening** We've all heard this before. As leaders, this may be one of our greatest challenges every hour of the day, but it's worth repeating. Listening requires patience.

- **Evaluating without Criticizing** Not every option is a good option. It takes patience to work through data to arrive at the best solution. This is especially true at the end of a quarter, or a new project launch. What does that look like in practice? Taking the time to hear options in a balanced and objective way—especially during meetings with people who tend to frustrate us.

The value of leadership Patience What's the value to us as leaders? We build deeper trust with our team members because they know, beyond a shadow of a doubt, that we are attentive to their thoughts. We become known for our ability to evaluate rival opinions, without damaging the reputations of others; demonstrating impartiality. We gain the respect of those around us for doing what others could not do, as we show restraint in difficult situations. Most likely, we will get better solutions from those we work with, simply because they will not fear criticism, reprisal, or belittlement. In short, we are modeling what we expect in others. Finally, it allows us to gain the high ground when we *must* place demands on our teams. By regularly demonstrating leadership patience as a characteristic of our style, we can more readily say to the team, *"We need to move, and we need to move quickly,"* when unforeseen situations compel us to act under the pressures we face.

It takes patience to build patience This is not an easy behavior to learn or practice - but it is critical for success. In the long run, the persona we project determines the effectiveness of our leadership; so, be patient. Take a breath. Reframe the conversation. Do whatever is necessary. Your people will thank you, and your leadership will become legendary. We live in an impatient world. While leadership patience is emotionally expensive, leadership impatience is costly.

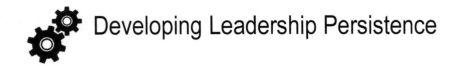# Developing Leadership Persistence

I recall an instance when I was so angry with someone in a business meeting, I literally wanted to punch him. I had been traveling for weeks, with little sleep, and I was under incredible stress in my new role. The individual across from me challenged me again and again, taunting me into a confrontation. I felt the weakness of the physical stress, but I knew I had to win the situation for the sake of my team (not to mention I ran the risk of rightful termination if I acted on my impulse—but it was *very* tempting).

I looked at the Vice-President across from me and asked, "Would you mind if I stepped out for just a minute?" He could tell I had reached a limit, and he said, "No problem." I walked out, splashed some cold water on my face, took a deep breath, and prayed. Having calmed down, I was ready to work through the situation; and I did. Had I given in at that moment and agreed to this demands of this individual, my team would have been put into a terrible situation, my credibility as a leader would have been reduced, and it is likely we would have failed. As Shakespeare wrote (and Vince Lombardi quoted): "Fatigue makes cowards of us all." While stress is a reality in leadership, persistence is mandatory.

When leaders give up, others follow. Whether leaders like it or not, we are a constant model of behavior to others. Every act we perform—in meetings, in our speech, in our time management, in the way we travel, in our apparel, in our exercise of judgment/favoritism, and in our demeanor—we are modeling behavior, and our behavior in persistence is a critical link in team success.

Hard truth #1—Leaders are being observed. It begins when we're young, and we watch how those in positions of authority react or respond to situations, and it continues until we die. We demand much from those who would show us the way to go; those who will engage the precious time of our lives in their endeavors. Those who would lead are in the spotlight, and their behavior influences others. Thus, as leaders, we need ways to demonstrate endurance in the midst of stress. This skill is even more critical in a day where any and all actions are immediately available in the virtual world. Because when leaders give up, others follow.

Hard truth #2—Leaders are only human. Leaders become physically exhausted; emotionally wrung out from personal matters that we cannot separate from our daily work, and from the day-to-day grind of dealing with non-stop problems, issues, and workplace challenges.

Here are a few things I have observed along the way:

Leadership Persistence is sometimes lost through problems *we create for ourselves.*

- **Favoritism** of individuals invariably leads to unnecessary conflict within a team. Favoritism creates an unnecessary emotional battle that drains precious energy.

- **Lack of attention to detail** is one of those things that can create chaos for us down the road. I've seen it; I've done it. *Don't cut corners.*

- **We foster unnecessary personal conflicts** that yield little organizational effectiveness.

Physical challenges wear us down. We all know what they are: lack of sleep, inadequate diet, excessive alcohol, travel, lack of exercise. I'm not here to preach about these things - every leader is aware of them, but they do need to be managed.

There are rapid ways to refresh under stress. As the story above shows, cold water can work wonders. There are ways to take exceptionally brief naps, or a quick walk outside; ways to experience a brain vacation during a meeting (yes, they are possible!). All can contribute to a quick moment of relief that buys us a fresh level of attention and clarity. On a personal note: As a Baby Boomer, one of my greatest mistakes as a leader was not taking real vacations. Time waits for no one. I regret those lost days.

Social challenges wear us down. Many of us in leadership roles have to deal with people on a non-stop basis. We don't get to choose the crisis—it chooses us, and it often comes in the form of people issues: conflict between team members, uncommitted leaders who are necessary to get the job done, and meetings, meetings, meetings.

One key element of managing social stress has to do with whether you are an extrovert or and introvert. Spending less time with people is essential if you are normally an introvert—critical for me, especially during days of business meetings. There are simple ways to "disappear," if only for a moment. Take a different hallway, find an unused meeting room, or disappear into a crowd when you are exhausted from too much people interaction. Moments matter. Above all, beware the naysayers. They are the great motivation drainers. Beware of them at all costs, unless they truly intend to help with your project or career. I find it is also bene-

> *ficial to carefully select (and spend time with) people who will naturally energize you; people who are interesting, people who are mentors, and people who share a passion for living. Hang around them as much as possible, and be one of them for others!*

Emotional challenges wear us down. Clearly, there are elements of our personal lives that we cannot partition off from our work lives. In my own circumstance, at one time I was dealing with a very close family member battling cancer, while managing a major project. The news was devastating. The pressures were immense, both personally and professionally.

> *There is a moment to explain, very clearly, to one's manager, "I have a difficult situation to manage." Make it plain; make it clear; make it known to those who can help. They will, but they must also get the job done. I witnessed workplace kindnesses during this situation, and I was grateful for the help, yet I knew they relied on my leadership to complete what I had been hired to do. I believe leaders can manage through these situations, and, in truth, sometimes work is a welcome relief from the pressure of great personal strain. There is a strange balance between being "heroic" and making the personal a daily drama for others to deal with (not recommended), versus completely ignoring the situation, as if it was not part of one's life. Neither extreme is effective. Persisting in the face of personal life struggles has an impact on others. Remember, they're watching how you manage the situation, and they gain strength from your strength in the face of hardship. Just don't use it as an excuse for cutting corners or ineffective workplace performance.*

My personal methods for increasing leadership persistence:

The great source of persistence is purpose. Perhaps my greatest personal act of leader persistence was attending night school, helping to raise three kids, working on an old (100 years) house, and holding down a full-time job—all at the same time. I didn't need the Ph.D. for my job, but I knew it was something I needed to do. The long term goal of going to night school (walking to parking lots on -10 degree January nights and scraping windows off my car, only to rise for work 10 hours later) seemed crazy at times, but the purpose remained. I needed to complete the achievement—not for others, but for myself; to demonstrate to myself that it could be done. Your personal purpose will take you far into the land of persistence. Life purposes are marathons, not sprints.

I rely on ancient wisdom to get me through my current problems. Finding books that have stood the test of time reminds me that some things can endure well beyond our physical limits. *Paradise Lost* is a favorite, along with Shakespeare, and *I love* very old theology. Dead authors have a way of inspiring like none else, and their words can provide that one moment of courage when all else fails. More than once I have had to give myself this speech: "He that hath no stomach to this fight, let him depart!"
~Shakespeare, St. Crispin's Day Speech, HENRY V.

Then again, sometimes I listen to rock and roll as loud as the stereo will go! Find your purpose and your inspiration, and you will find your persistence.

Elements of Leadership Wisdom

Gaining leadership wisdom—a lifetime pursuit. Over time, through demanding projects, difficult experience, terrible failures, and outrageous achievements, leaders gain wisdom. Here are elements of leadership wisdom I have observed after working with thousands of people over the past four decades.

The Individual Level

- **Wise leaders accept imperfection in themselves and others.** No one is perfect. No one bats 1.000. Wise leaders accept this important fact.

- **They do the best they can with what they have.** No leader has everything they want and, very often, they don't even have things they need. No matter. Wise leaders figure it out, and do the best they can with what is at hand.

- **They help turn pain into victory.** The truly wise assess the deepest needs of their team members and, *though they are wise enough not become counselors or psychotherapists*, they draw the difficulties of people's lives into something that heals and builds.

The Group Level

- **They balance imperfection in others with the need to get the job done.** Accepting the fact that everyone (including the leader) has imperfections does not hinder the achievement of the end goal. Care does not imply apathy. Wise leaders run businesses, not country clubs.

- **They have the ability to see and share a vision.** Sensing a vision for the future is a tool available to some, but not all. This is leadership wisdom at its deepest moment—to be the prophet of something that does not exist, and to bring such clarity to others that *they, too,* can see what is ahead.

- **They have the ability to draw out the emotional power of motivation in others.** Motivation is not dispensed by leaders through pep talks, speeches, or other transitory events. Motivation is drawn from the cores of individuals seeking purpose in their lives.

- **They have the wisdom to know when people have had enough.** Leaders have an "entropy meter" that flashes red when they sense their people need a break. Rare are the times when a leader needs to push people into the RED ZONE for long stretches. Rarer still are the careers of leaders who do.

- **They have the wisdom to put the right pieces in the right place.** The wise among us can see the broken pieces; the disconnected sections; the non-fitting parts. We can orchestrate them into something beautiful; something elegant and powerful; something influential; and, something that endures.

The Organizational Level

- **They recognize unnecessary organizational chaos.** The unruliness of wasteful, disruptive organizational chaos is not a friend to the wise leader.

- **They have the wisdom to effectively assemble a team.** Team building is known by its results, not by its seminars. Wise leaders know how to bring each personality into place for winning, not through Myer-Briggs, nor through any manipulative personality inventories, but through drawing together the right skills to match the need at hand.

- **Wise leaders have the ability to stoke motivational fires through their own example.** While wise leaders neither denigrate themselves, nor overestimate their abilities; they are keenly aware of how their presence builds motivational fire. They know how to manage presence without excessive ego. People respond to them because of their deep integrity, their passion for the work, their ability to listen, and their life focus and discipline.

Lofty? Yes. Possible? Yes. Worth striving for? Absolutely. Wise leaders make history, and their names are remembered long after they retire from business and have departed from this earth.

The Power of Leadership Courage

In every leader's life, there are moments calling for personal strength and conviction beyond the routine. There are times when managers, directors, and leaders of all varieties must simply stand firm in unpleasant settings to ensure the success of the organization. The downside is simple: exercising leadership courage can put us in a spot where we are challenging sacred projects of powerful leaders, and thus place us in a precarious, and sometimes unpleasant, organizational situation. And yet, leadership courage is needed for organizations to succeed.

I define **Leadership Courage** as the willingness to state an unpopular truth, which may cause personal risk. The amount of leadership courage required is proportional to the number of people who will be adversely affected by the truth—especially those who are of higher rank in an organization.

What moments require this sort of courage?
- When a costly project is sorely off track, and likely to get worse without intervention.
- When an employee has been put into an awkward circumstance by leaders with much more power (I am not referring to harassment, I am referring to leaders asking employees to make decisions that are well above their pay grade, because leaders don't want to make a decision).
- When no one else in the room will state what everyone knows to be the truth:
  - *The project is going to take three times as long as planned.*
  - *Incorrect assumptions made at the beginning of the*

project must be brought to light.
- *The wrong people are on the team, and their incompetence is bringing about failure.*
- *The budget is out of whack.*
- *Customers are complaining in droves.*

Some cautions:

- **Raw honesty sometimes causes others to cringe and run for the exits.** I have seen people make harsh statements about a project without considering diplomacy and professionalism. Even bad news needs to be delivered without drama.

- **Know your stuff.** If you shoot your mouth off without facts, you'll be heading for the exit (or at least some backwater job) for a long time.

- **Don't repeat Old News.** If you're just into grandstanding by repeating the obvious, you're not being courageous—you're being stupid. I've seen the reactions of executives when someone sounds the alarm for a fire that has already been put out; it does not go well.

- **Make an effort to minimize the Ego Damage you're going to inflict.** Somewhere in your messaging, you need to balance the bad news with elements of success.

- **Be prepared for some backlash.** Courageous acts aren't always followed by pats on the back—at least, not initially.

What's in it for you? Why take the risk!?
Not all, but many, of the people I have worked for over the past decades actually *welcome* truth. They want to know the

risks inherent in a situation, so they can mitigate disaster.

Respectful Leadership Courage is admired by upper level executives—they live it every day, or they're gone. When they see you exhibiting leadership courage, they'll see some of their own risk taking behavior.

Done properly, your courage will build you a reputation as someone who cares deeply about the success of your organization, and is willing to put the organization ahead of self-interest, not to mention the self-respect you'll gain knowing you've done everything you could do to help the organization succeed. There's a deep gratification in truth, and organizations must stand on truth to move forward.

The Power of Managerial Presence

We hear about managerial authenticity a lot, these days. I fear it will become a buzzword like all the buzzword predecessors that have been overworked these past few years, including "engagement" and "empowerment." There is too much at stake with the word "authenticity" to allow it to become a cliché in management.

Authenticity is Managerial Presence, and yet, perhaps we need a concrete definition of the word. What is authenticity? What does that mean in concrete terms? In my opinion, managerial authenticity is part of a cluster of behavioral and character traits I call *managerial presence*.

Here's how I define Managerial Presence:
•Tactful emotional interaction.
•Logical persuasion through dialogue and listening.
•Sacrificial engagement for the wider organizational cause.
•Appreciating a person as they are, while projecting expectations of what they can become in their role, under our leadership.

Tactful emotional interaction is a complex psychological process requiring emotional investment in the people we lead. It goes beyond delegation and barking orders. It means we *care enough to understand a subordinate beyond their title, role, or task*. Empathy would be a corollary, but not quite the same. In business, we are not present to be counselors or psychotherapists—that's not our job—but we can engage at a level much deeper than merely "get the job done."

Logical persuasion through dialogue and listening is the cognitive investment of raising an argument through reason and data, and *modeling* a rational approach to the discussion.

We demonstrate how human interaction can be successful by demonstrating successful interactions.

Sacrificial engagement for the wider organizational "cause" is the intentional expenditure of effort, energy, time, and finances to demonstrate our *commitment* to the person. This, in my view, is the heart of authenticity - going the extra mile for another team member; sacrificial leadership is authentic leadership.

Appreciating a person *as they are,* while projecting expectations of what they can become in their role, under our leadership. This element of Managerial Presence transcends gender, power, diversity, ethnicity and socioeconomic status. It simply means acknowledging the person with respect as they are—no strings attached. But, as managers, we also own the responsibility of bringing people forward through coaching and expectation setting.

We don't need to read hundreds of leadership books to achieve Managerial Presence. We need to live it. People can sense Managerial Presence:

• When we are taking the time to truly understand a problem from another person's perspective.
• When we switch our plan because their plan is superior to ours.
• When humor increases the energy of the team because we didn't take ourselves too seriously.
• When a sacrifice of time, or the investment of serious coaching activity and effort, is the event that changes the course of the project. This can be done—all it takes is the will to do so.

Managing It All and Staying Sane

Every day, every leader is torn in a hundred (a thousand?) different directions. I hear this from nearly every leader I meet. Every time one fire goes out, another one starts. The world is filled with non-stop distractions, both personal and professional. And with different styles of management come fresh means of disruption, not to mention customer challenges, employee grievances and frustrations, along with the occasional unforeseen consequence. How to manage it all? Careful management of your own physical, cognitive, motivational, and emotional energy are the keys to managing work life, and you can do that through some personal disciplines in the workplace.

Managing Emotional Energy The key here is: don't create problems for yourself.

• Unnecessary strife at work yields nothing but long term emotional drag. Don't start a fight that doesn't move things forward.
• Cutting corners causes issues down the road.
• There is safety in a good plan, even if it isn't perfect. Don't allow yourself to get so trapped on the treadmill that you can't take a moment to reflect, cut a few things off the list, and regroup.

When things get a little tense, check your motivational energy

Managing Motivational Energy Here, you need to manage your Proximal and Distal Goals—cool words, eh? They're not just academic, they're very valuable! Goal setting theorists talk about two kinds of goals: Proximal and Distal, with proximal being fairly immediate, and distal meaning *distant*!

- Take the longest view. Ask yourself, "Is this effort making a difference *in my life?*" That view will help you prioritize how much motivational effort to apply to a situation (and whether to self-select *out* of the situation).

- Is this effort developing my skills, strength, and confidence? Even in the most difficult of circumstances, I have always found a way to explain how I am benefiting from the greatest drudgery or mind-numbing speech. Sound self - serving? I suppose, but then again, the only person managing my career and life is *me!*

Why do this? There is a deep sense of satisfaction knowing that even the most difficult, frustrating and awful circumstances can be used for something greater down the road. It's a way to tell yourself, "I can use this experience for something in my career." Ninety percent of the time, that statement is true. *(Lying to yourself the other 10% will keep your sanity while you're regrouping.)*

Managing Cognitive energy The key here: take control of what you can truly manage.

- Stay out of the details until you need them. Details are cognitively demanding—we all know that. Cognitive loading causes people to tire quickly, and to get frustrated. Watch for strategic rabbit trails during meetings—the guy or gal who decides they want to work out every detail, instead of dealing with the problem at hand.

- Refocusing people back to the original goal is one key step in keeping priorities straight. I recall a situation with an internationally known consultant working with a group of very high powered leaders who all had "input." The main tool he used to keep them on track was continually reminding them of the primary goal.

- Help your mind mind the details. The human mind simply cannot manage thousands of details. Cognitive psychologists speak of "schemas;" that is, compartments in the mind where things fit. Whether you use paper (old school, like me), or some whiz-bang fancy hi-tech item (which may or may not work when you need it, btw) you need a system of categorization to manage the thousands of details you encounter every year. Then when the details come up, you have a place to put them!

Orderliness of material makes it easier for you to manage the details. Use categories of work to sort things out; in other words, organize your life in a simple way that allows you to drop the latest detail into place, so you don't forget it, but in a place you can find it quickly. And, of course, there are those nasty computers, cell phones, pagers, and instant messages draining energy—but, it's your choice whether to respond, right?

Managing Physical Energy Here, watch for weird physical energy drains. Our physical bodies demand water, food, and rest. In the business world, it's odd that we rarely pay attention to these demands. We just keep on going until we're exhausted. I don't think many companies want their people to be exhausted, but companies also don't manage people's lives, *we do*. So:

- Find meeting rooms that have enough space for people.

- Pick light snacks. (One of my former training coordinators used to order heavy pasta and bread for lunch for my participants. That was great around 2 in the afternoon...)
- Find ways to eliminate irritating noises, lights, distractions of all sorts.
- Find a more comfortable chair.

There is *always* a way; however, when all else fails, put down the briefcase and cell phone and, finally, when it looks like there is no hope for success, remember these words of my father: *"Tomorrow is another day."*

It works wonders.

Organizational Awareness: The Seventh Sense

I recall the time one of my former co-workers, a Vice-President of Service, said to me, "You can feel the buzz in the branch." He was referring to different teams he had visited along the way in his travels across a large US business. Here's what he meant:

You walk into a room and look around. You listen. You hear. You read the faces. You can tell within minutes, maybe seconds, whether the team is ready to go, or is in tough shape. This is the seventh sense of leadership.

Organizational awareness: what is it?

It is nearly impossible to train or teach someone how to develop this sense, since it is something beyond standard management practices of finance, contracts, and operations. It is a combination of emotional intelligence, deep experience, intuition, and gut feel. It is a seventh sense, the ability to quickly grasp what is working and what is destined for failure, with accuracy and with boldness. Call it insight, but whatever it is, *it is an essential part of effective leadership.*

Inside your organization right now, there is someone who rarely complains about anything, whose team consistently achieves greatness, whose team you hear virtually no complaints about. Why would that be the case? It is very likely they have this skill. They have the seventh sense of organizational awareness.

If you have this skill, be grateful. If not, find someone who has it and hire them.

How do you know if you have the seventh sense?

Frankly, I don't know if someone can train the seventh sense until they see an example of it, or learn the benefits. It may be something that's built during childhood. Among other things, *organizational awareness is taking fear and turning it into action.*

- Do you have a wide angle lens on the people you work with? Can you see how they fit together (or don't fit together)?
- When you see something brewing that could potentially go wrong, do you wait until the last minute, stand to the side expecting someone else to correct a situation, or do you engage a team to fix the issue?
- Can you read negative "vibes" in a room? (Do you know when things are out of sync and people have put up barriers and walls?) And, if so, do you move to correct the situation?
- When you see something that could work to everyone's advantage, do you act, or let the opportunity slide?
- When you have a good idea, do you write it down and bring your team into the concept, or just let it vanish into the ether?

How do you gain this seventh sense?

- Trust your gut. If you sense something is wrong, take the time to think it through. Something *is* wrong—you just need to figure it out. Trust your gut: if it can go wrong, it probably will, so *act* on your awareness.

- Watch other effective leaders as they navigate difficult waters—what do they do?
- Allow disciplined spontaneity; a contradiction in terms? No. There is a place to be spontaneous in emotionally responding to someone within the boundaries of appropriate organizational behavior.
- Read everything you can to increase insight, including good fiction.

The seventh sense - it's all about observing people and their reaction to situations, and *responding for the benefit of the organization.*

This sense is built over the years from paying close attention to experience, consequences, and achievement but, most of all, by being a keen observer of human behavior. Watch, learn, absorb, and remember. Leadership is much, much more than numbers and projects. Leadership, in its finest form, is organizational awareness in action.

Leaders Will Often Be Wrong, and That's What's Right

No matter what we do as leaders, we will always have our critics. To change anything is to invite criticism. Agreeableness may be a part of the Big Five inventory of personality (Big 5 trait theory), but if we are agreeable to everything and everyone, we are not leaders; we are merely everyone's acquaintance or friend. And, as we all know, friendships are not designed to "get the job done," they're designed to help us recover from getting the job done.

Facing our critics is not easy in any arena. The moments of self-doubt, the second-guessing we go through, the sleepless nights; they are all part of our craft and often a result of intense criticism. Leaders will often be wrong, but in my view, that's what makes them right.

We often don't have all the answers, we're sometimes unsure of where we're going, and we may find problems in our idea that may create more work and stress for others, but those on the sidelines have the luxury of tearing apart our ideas and watching for the flaws, the incomplete strands of thought, and the dangers of the risks we have not considered. They will nitpick an idea to death if we let them!

Anytime we assert a new idea as leaders, we are open targets for criticism. If we do our work well, we should be able to answer the *skeptics* and win them over, but I doubt we will ever manage the *cynics,* whose very lives are built around standing on the sidelines tearing apart good ideas. **No matter.**

"Sticks and stones" are no match for harsh words and demeaning attitudes. We must get past the emotional turmoil of rejection, criticism, and downright abuse of our ideas if we are to be successful.

"The dogs bark, but the caravan moves on."

What does matter is our own passion. The fuel of our own passion to make something greater, to move the needle and change something, is our source of overcoming the critics. In the end, all but the harshest and unbending critic will often grudgingly admit our victories and successes.

Passion will overcome doubt. What we want to achieve, in the end, will override even the most monstrous and withering criticisms of our work. We know where we're going. We will get there. We will persist.

I have always loved the Arab Proverb "The dogs bark, but the caravan moves on." How brilliantly it states what we, as leaders, must face on our journey to great achievements.

Press on my fellow leaders.

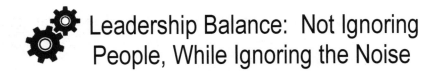 # Leadership Balance: Not Ignoring People, While Ignoring the Noise

In any leadership challenge, we are faced with myriad inputs, ideas, thoughts, recommendations, prophets of doom, new concepts, sarcastic looks, cynical emails, executive pressure to conform, and a cacophony of endless advice.

The value of organizational input is obvious: by listening, we gain crucial insight, but that doesn't mean we need to listen to all the noise.

We can learn from those on the ground, the very people who are facing the battle every day. Although they may have insight, they may also be wrong. They have a very slanted view of day-to-day activities, based on their current emotional pain. Leaders listen, but do not base their long-term plans on short-term emotional pain.

We can learn from those who had different experiences in the past. Let's face it; experience matters! The things people have done in the past are legitimate, concrete situations they can point to and say, "See, this is what happens when you ..." And yet, if we simply rely on those with a bad experience, we are likely to be pulled by the emotional tug of a wounded victim.

We can learn from the guru with the latest technology! In other words, input from the future. Technology reigns supreme these days, in most circles. Ignoring the techies of the world is simply stupid. People with good technical sense can make the world (our world—your world) a better place, but technology for the sake of technology is never a good idea. Still, there are those who want to try every new thing that hits the cloud!

We can learn from our peers who have done similar projects. I find this group to be the most effective of the bunch, simply because they've had to navigate tough waters in the same organization, yet even they may have a somewhat jaded view of the situation, simply because they lead a different team or *their own leadership methods were ineffective*. (Not all leaders are equal.)

So, what's a leader to do!? Listen, but ignore the noise.

• A great starting point is admitting that no one, and I mean no one has *the* solution. As a leader, it's your job to weigh all the ingredients and build a solution.

• Listen most carefully to those who are truly interested in your success—people who have a track record of investing in your career; those who want you to succeed.

• Listen for the real kernel of truth from those who are most frustrated. Somewhere in their rant is a gemstone of warning.

• Acknowledging to yourself that your decisions and approach will not make everyone happy. It just won't happen.

Early in my first supervisory role, I had a conversation with my boss. I told him I was going to go and talk to everyone about a decision I made to make sure everyone would like it. He asked me, "Have you thought this through?" I answered,

"Yes." "Have you considered the different angles of your decision?" Again, I answered, "Yes." "Have you done your best?" "Yes," I replied. "Then you need to move forward with your decision."

At the end of the day, no leader will be right all the time, and while we need not ignore people, we *must* ignore the noise.

SECTION I
SELF LEADERSHIP
Tools, Techniques & Hot Spots

HOT SPOTS

Career Wake-Up Calls

You've traveled extensively. Sometimes, you've had the luxury of someone calling you in your hotel room with a gentle voice saying, "It's 6 a.m." Bleary-eyed from last night's networking event and presentation, you arise and prepare for the day. *Or not.*

Maybe it just seems a bit too early, and you think to yourself, "A bit more rest will help me do better work today." Then, you go back to sleep. You ignored the wake-up call. A few hours later: disaster. You've missed your flight, a conference call, an important meeting, or critical family contact while you're on the road. Not good. Not good at all. You ignored the wake up call. *Disaster.*

Organizational settings provide wake up calls, too. You may want to scan this list of alarms and assess whether these situations ring true for you.

Lazy leadership from too much time in one Role

After several years (decades?), you've mastered the role you're in. In fact, you're coasting. You know it. What's worse is you're rewarded for your skill and expertise. It's a comfy place. No need to exert too much energy to maintain.

- **Alarm Bell:** If you're that comfortable, the situation is running on its own, and other leaders know it. During times of change, they also know *you're not really needed*, because you're not doing anything important.

Personal Stagnation

You're no longer growing intellectually. You don't read leadership or management materials. You stopped taking classes a long time ago. You're stagnant, and what's worse is *you don't really care* because the job requires such little energy, and it provides you time for other personal pursuits.

- **Alarm Bell:** If you're giving the same old answers, and talking about the same "low hanging fruit" you've spoken of for five years, be aware that others sense your stagnation, too.

Sloppiness in the Details

You find yourself lacking data at critical moments, but demonstrate little concern. (In the words of 14 year old teens everywhere, your attitude is: "*Whatever!*") Other departments who rely on your work find themselves having to rework things you've sent them.

- **Alarm Bell:** If others cannot rely on your levels of accuracy, you are no longer a trustworthy team member; thus, you are expendable.

Personal Performance Wake-up Calls

You've noticed your performance reviews are mediocre, at best, yet you find yourself unmoved—even apathetic and cynical. "*Performance appraisals are just a company procedure. They don't really mean anything. We're just checking the box here.*"

- **Alarm Bell:** During times of severe organizational stress, performance ratings are some of the only "hard data" a company will turn to when downsizing. You can argue that the process is subjective, unfair, or biased all day, but it will not change the results.

Cutting ethical corners in other's performance Failure

If you find yourself approving, or gently modifying, numbers portrayed as "truth," and you're overlooking it, you're on a gentle slope to disaster.

- **Alarm Bell:** Ethical violations become evident over time and they cause irreparable career havoc. They become public record.

Personal Hubris

"These people need me. I'm the expert. I'm the head of the tribe, with all the tribal knowledge. I'm the one who makes this place effective. They cannot get along without me." These words have been said by thousands of displaced, misguided leaders who held an illusion of their own importance.

- **Alarm Bell:** Everyone is expendable. *Everyone.* You're not that important. Time to wake up.

Now and then, it's wise for us to do an assessment of the wake-up calls we've heard. Every leader is vulnerable to these risks—for a hundred reasons, and sometimes for no reason. Could be low energy, a boss we do not like, a job we abhor, or team members who are a constant strain. No matter. Some of these alarms only ring once. In this extremely competitive world we live in, our careers are the only thing we can manage.

Hear the wake up call: *"Other people are waiting for your job."* Now is the time to reset the clock.

Leadership Blind Spots

The most important thing I learned in Driver's Education was *"check your blind spot."* Candidly, that bit of coaching has literally saved my life multiple times throughout the past several decades. Not checking a blind spot can mean destruction while driving a car, but I often wonder whether leaders take the time to check their blind spots. What you can't see can hurt you, and others.

Here are a few blind spots I have observed in others and, in the interest of authenticity, some which others have brought to my attention over the years:

"My way or the highway" Power has a way of increasing this blind spot. *Unidirectional leadership is an oxymoron.* While leaders may think this approach demonstrates leadership, they may be losing the very followers they need to be successful.

"I don't need any feedback." Those who do not want to hear about dangerous flaws that may be impeding their success are especially vulnerable to this blind spot. Think "ego on steroids." As the old Proverb says: *"Pride comes before a fall."* Feedback is the great blind spot remover. We don't need to listen to every Tom, Dick and Harriet that comes our way, but trusted feedback can prevent career damage and accidents.

Feigned commitment Leaders who nod their heads in approval during key meetings, but only do so for appearances, are sending a message of disinterestedness, which damages credibility.

An unwillingness to get one's hands dirty when the chips are down Leaders who are *"above all that"* send a powerful message about their true concern for the challenges facing their team.

Demonstrating an "illusion of participation" In change management and organizational development, we coach people to refrain from asking people for input unless they plan to use the input (Think employee surveys, for example). Leaders erode follower confidence in their sincerity when they act as if they're interested in someone's advice without including those thoughts in a solution. Loss of sincerity = loss of trust = loss of influence.

Assuming others know what we know Sometimes, leaders think about a decision for days, weeks, even months; but, when they decide to act, they forget that their team has not had the time to process what they've been thinking about, causing confusion and frustration in the ranks.

"Failure to communicate" Sometimes, leaders are so busy they simply don't take the time to follow-up on communications they may have sent forth–emails, speeches, and even corporate announcements. Part of the reason this occurs is because leaders may believe face-to-face communications will take too long. I offer this: five minutes of clarity can launch immense employee energy. People don't need hours of communications–they need clear communications.

Falling for the "shiny new object" Leaders can fall for the distractions of novelty, but when they lose interest in something they started, their example influences many others.

Leader distraction becomes an organizational distraction. I call it Organizational Attention Deficit Disorder .

Undervaluing our coworkers We sometimes unwittingly categorize people and place them in mental boxes. We can become dismissive of those who have not attained our rank. As leaders, we often struggle through heavy workloads and MBA graduate courses to reach the top of the ladder. It is tempting to dismiss those who have not accomplished what we've achieved, yet people sense (and remember) dismissive and condescending behavior toward them. The challenge with this blind spot is we do not know what the future holds for them or for us. It is possible we may be working for them one day...

Blind spots can be remedied with candid leader openness to criticism that articulates the danger of the blind spot; the short-term impact of the blind spot, as well as the long-term, career-damaging blind spots that can run someone off course forever. One or two trusted colleagues can provide great insight to leadership blind-spots.

What are your leadership blind spots? Have you considered what they might be? Have you asked for true criticism of your style by a trusted colleague? We can learn from the experiences of others, and improve our leadership, as we discover our own blind spots.

How Executives Create Organizational Craziness

The reality no one seems to want to talk about

I recall a conversation with someone in a branch office many years ago. We were discussing a new change program and I was asking for his help. Then, he pointed to the stack of brochures, letters, and reports on his desk. They were all from the Corporate offices (yes, that plural is intentional). He looked at me and said, "I have to decide which of these people are going to be frustrated that I did not work on their program." *(He used different words which are not appropriate for this book, but use your imagination.)* He was trying to balance the incredible demands of a disconnected corporate engine that manufactured programs he was required to implement. In short, corporate was making him crazy.

The Strange Truth: Leadership is the driving force of Organizational Craziness

When people are hired into leadership roles, they have to make *their* mark. That means they will enlist every ounce of creative energy, available financial resources, and organizational focus to realize their own accomplishments. So far, so good. One major program sent to the field provides focus and allows people to dig in and make it happen.

Now, multiply that program times ten, and you get the picture. HR, Finance, Legal, Operations, Sales, Engineering and Product Development, Marketing, Communications, Public Relations—they all develop programs. But we're not finished yet. Flying high above these groups are teams developing Lean Processes that cover entire Divisions, and above all that are the recurring organizational reorganizations. Every one of the leaders driving these programs wants to make their mark. Then it's time to install a new ERP system. Get the picture? I know you do.

Each of the initiatives and programs (though not all) likely has great merit and value to the corporation. It is the aggregate that makes organizations crazy.

New Kid on the Block

Then there's a change of guard and everything gets flipped upside down! Here's what I mean: The new leader comes in to replace all the ostensibly bad policies of the former leader, throwing the organization into yet more chaos.

When this happens, and the organization is turned upside down, employees get agitated, and their progress begins to slow. People seek predictability, not chaos.

Here's what happens at the Ground Level

- **Silos: great for farms, but not for corporations.** Organizations often become siloed for the reasons I listed above. Departments focus on their own needs to the exclusion of the success of others, because there are resource constraints of even the most powerful and financially successful companies. Siloing behavior has a direct and significant negative impact on organizational output.

- **Too much stuff makes people defocused.** Even the best managers become defocused because of excessive (and sometimes conflicting) initiatives. Too much at one time drives people crazy and makes them ineffective.

- **Too much stuff causes directional uncertainty.** People are sometimes uncertain about how their work fits into organizational success, exacerbating ineffectiveness and causing employee anxiety, employee concern, wait-and-see attitudes, and social loafing. *The very programs leaders implement actually stall the success they hope to achieve!*

- **The reality of "Breathing Dinosaurs"** One of the worst side effects of all these programs is that ineffective projects and programs are left in place, draining precious organizational time and energy. One executive I talked with said, "All these processes create organizational sediment and sludge—it slows things down." These programs remain in place because they are the fair-haired children of executives and leaders who want to make a mark.

- **Everything is priority #1** This can only happen in parallel universes. Something must take second priority.

- **"You can't handle the truth!"** People will default to what makes them successful. One branch manager told me, "You know what I think about? I think about my bonus at the end of the year, and I ignore everything that doesn't help me make my numbers." This is the hard reality about excessive programs.

- **Where is the Air Traffic Controller?** Great leaders know when they are creating organizational craziness, and they reassess priorities. They take time for a "clean up in aisle seven." Call it housekeeping, call it rebooting—whatever you call it, great leaders know when it's time to stop some things and focus on the critical few.

Leadership craziness leads to
Organizational Attention Deficit Disorder

Researchers say this about ADD: "The core symptoms...are developmentally inappropriate levels of inattention, hyperactivity, and impulsivity." In other words, a person is not paying attention, is overactive in their behavior, and acting impulsively. Sound familiar? Bohn's definition of Organizational Attention Deficit Disorder: *An organization's unwillingness and inability to focus on the critical few; accepting any and all projects as worthy of first-priority effort, resulting in employee burnout and organizational ineffectiveness.*

What leaders can do: Sometimes, for the sake of the organization, leaders just need to say "No." The most important thing leaders can do to alleviate this challenge is the very thing they expect of their people: *Work together with others as a team.* I realize that's a tall order, but the challenges I listed will not go away when disconnected programs continue to pile up on those who do the work. Disciplined management provides maximum goal clarity, manages priorities, maintains focus for the team, and stays the course to ensure the right things get done.

The accelerated pace of organizational change is unlikely to slow anytime soon, but that doesn't mean everything needs to change at one time.

Finishing What You Started:
The Hardest Part

The enthusiasm of a new organizational change wears thin after the going gets rough but, as leaders, we need to stay the course until the change is complete. By far the toughest part of a leader's work is to *finish the change* and ensure it is part of your organizational structure. As a leader, you're the *Architect of Change*, but you may be called upon to do some finish carpentry.

Organizational Barriers to completion

Unforeseen circumstances Loss of resources is a sure-fire way to prevent the change from becoming part of the organization. Ensuring that the team has everything they need to finish the project should be a key concern for you and your team.

Organizational Attention Deficit Disorder Organizational distractions can seriously hinder the completion of a change. Watch out for the new shiny object and avoid it!

Managerial Barriers to completion

Other priorities Take the leader away from the project; when managers see the leader leave, it's a drain on morale. A successful change leader told me, "Leaders need to lead from the front, be visible, and communicate with confidence on point."

Leader boredom The greatest temptation to having others lose interest in a critical change project is when the leader moves on to something else.

Assuming the project is done This is a misguided action on the part of the leader. Leaders need to know categorically, indisputably, and without qualification that the project is done, done, done!

Individual Barriers to completion

Frustration The "grind" of the project wears people out. The long term expenditure of physical, mental, cognitive, and emotional energy causes people to lose hope and lose heart. In short, they get tired of working on the project. Setbacks are particularly tough on team members—especially setbacks that could have been avoided through better upfront diagnosis. *Hint: Team energy lost must be team energy replaced!*

Distraction Shiny new objects are the bane of all projects. Remember that the current project, itself, was once a "shiny new object."

Your behavioral role in finishing the change

Persistence You are leading in more ways than through communication; your example matters. Persistence is omnipotent in the business world. People understand that when the leader stays the course to the end, they mean business; in other words, the change mattered to them. *If the change matters to you, the leader, it will matter to your organization.*

Clarity Reminding people of the "why?" is critical for completion. Constant clarity is essential throughout the project, but especially at the end, clarity makes all the difference: Here's why we started this; here's why we're working on this; here's the difference it is already making; here's what it will do for our company.

Recognition   Energy expended must be energy refilled. When the team works hard and gets things done, the leader must respond in kind, with hard work for the team! A bit of a partying is always a good encouragement along the way; better still, have pizza with the team to celebrate their current victories.

Communication to the end   Demonstrate what has happened as a result of their effort! Tell the *organization*, tell the *managers,* tell the *people* the results of the team effort.

Renewing vigor   Don't add work to the already busy team members, but show them some care along the way—they need it! The best way I have seen this done is when an executive comes out to have lunch with a team to discuss progress.

How will you know when you're finished?

"Are we there yet?" the small child asks. You won't know if you're done until you hear it from people who have lived through the change and came out smiling (or at least grudgingly excited!).

Revisiting Initial Metrics   At the beginning of a project, executives ask: "How will we know when we're done?" Remember those metrics you put in place at the beginning? Now is the time to test your theory.

Managerial Check-In   Have a meeting with your managers, and ask them how it's going. Have a face-to-face check-in to assess how things are going. What's happening with your groups? Is everyone on board?

Celebrate! When it's all said and done, celebrate! Make a big deal out of the success and the people who made it successful, because you may have to call on them in the future! *Now let's get this done.*

Is It Office Politics, or is It You?

I've heard many frustrated colleagues say this about their organizational culture: "It's not rocket science; it's political science." ...or is it? "Politics" is the default place to blame just about anything one doesn't like in the workplace, and the more one is passed over for promotions or perks or special projects, the more cynical they become, and the more likely they will view their corporation as "political." Candidly, I believe this issue will become an even greater challenge for the next generation of workers, *but what does "politics" really mean?*

Here's my definition: Politics in the workplace is generally a perception of favoritism or an abuse of power.

Politics looks like this at a personal level:

- I feel left out of a discussion.
- Decisions are being made without my input.
- I was passed over for a promotion, and someone else was promoted instead of me.
- There is obvious favoritism going on here that negatively impacts me.

Each of these statements is very ego-invested; in other words, we believe we were treated poorly because of some nefarious, clandestine, underhanded, stealth plot to damage our reputation and stall our career. "Politics" is an abuse of power? That simply may not be true. Here's why:

Power is a reality in the workplace. There is competition for jobs within a corporation. There is scarcity of resources and there are limited opportunities at the top. Jeffrey Pfeffer of

Harvard University wrote entire books on the subject of organizational power. It is a reality we cannot avoid.

Here are three views of power:

"Power corrupts, and absolute power corrupts absolutely."
~ Lord Acton

"Power has such a bad name that many good people persuade themselves they want nothing to do with it."
~ John Gardner

"Power...is the capacity to translate intention into reality and sustain it."
~Bennis and Nannus

Power looks much different at the organizational level.
Organizations simply cannot do everything they would like to do (nor should they). That means some people will not get their way (at this time, but maybe in the future). Decisions must be made, resources must be prioritized, and some projects must be jettisoned because they are ineffective. Team members are directly impacted by those decisions, and not everyone is going to be happy about it.

Organizations and groups are not immune from power conflicts, yet we tend to use the euphemism "politics" to describe the use and abuse of power in organizations. So as much as we would like, the use and abuse of power will not go away. *"Unless we are willing to come to terms with organizational power and influence, and admit that the skills of getting things done are as important as the skills of figuring out WHAT to do, our organizations will fall further and further behind."* (Pfeffer)

Time for a personal Reflection:
Did someone else get promoted because they were a better fit? More highly trained? Because they built a network and had better organizational connections? What's your track record of achievement? What's your work ethic? How are you making yourself visible in the corporation? Did you effectively make the pitch? Were you honestly the right person for the job? Time will tell.

How to remain focused if things seem tipped against you.
What are *your* goals in life? What do you want to attain? How do you see yourself fitting into your organization? How will you build a reputation for yourself that builds your own power of influence? What will you do to remove your own excuses for not achieving a desired role?

My personal Observations:
Someone who continually complains about politics is not likely to get the jobs and projects they seek. In short, their complaints will limit their effectiveness, and their long term cynicism will damage their teams. It's better to determine your own destiny in the workplace through achievement, success, effective networking, and good old hard work.

One of my former bosses said he hired me into a major project because I was not "political." To me, all that meant was this: I focused on getting the job done. That's the advice I would give anyone who wants to overcome the perception that organizational politics is managing your life. *Your career belongs to you and you alone.*

How Leaders Unravel the Invisible Fabric of Trust

Trust is the delicate, invisible fabric that holds all relationships together. Damage, cut, or fray one thread and the fabric quietly unravels.

In business, in relationships—both intimate and distant—in conversation, in government, in education (dare I mention places of worship?); throughout our lives, trust is the fabric that holds relationships together. Or not.

Here are some ways the invisible fabric of trust is unraveled. *(I know, because I have experienced and acted these behaviors. I am not here to throw stones, but to warn aspiring leaders.)*

Saying one thing; doing another: The fabric of trust is weakened when we act contrary to our words. Our words are an outward expression of our intentions, but if we say one thing and do another thing, it is hard for people to identify the real person behind the words. Uncertainty breeds wariness, another word for mistrust. While the loss of one thread may not matter a great deal, the dissonance between our words and actions over time causes more threads to unravel, and the fabric grows very, very weak.

Disingenuous speech: Words that reek of any "ism" are words that tear at the fabric of trust. What we say matters. Harsh words, abusive language, and sarcastic jokes in the presence of others do serious damage to the invisible fabric of trust.

Making promises that cannot be kept: Your track record is the measure of your credibility. Overpromising may make you look good in a meeting, but *incomplete projects are monuments, not trophies*. People know who will get things done, and they also know those who merely talk a good game. If you cannot fulfill your promises, you tear a gaping hole in the invisible fabric of trust. Young leaders are especially tempted to overpromise to get a name for themselves. Be careful not to damage your credibility too early in your career through this mistake.

Refusing to apologize after relationships have been damaged: The only possible way for a patch to be sewn on the fabric of trust is through a true apology. An apology can repair the fabric of trust but, like a piece of cloth, there will always be evidence that it was once torn.

There are many, many books on the value of trust in leadership, for good reason. For me, the greatest compliment anyone can provide in business is, "I trust you to get this done."

End of Section Personal Review

- **Does this Section address a part of your leadership/ management style that you need to improve on?**

Notes_____

_____

_____

_____

- **Do you need to share a chapter in this book with a col- league?**

Notes_____

_____

_____

_____

- **Does this Section address an issue that relates to your workplace?**

Notes_____

_____

_____

_____

- **Is there advice in this Section that would be helpful to implement in your workplace?**

Notes_____

_____

_____

_____

SECTION II
TEAM LEADERSHIP
Tools, Techniques & Hot Spots

TOOLS

Assess Your Team Leadership Skills With Two Tough Questions

Team effectiveness is a result of two things: how well your people work together, and how well they work with others in the organization. As a leader, you are responsible for managing both elements of team effectiveness.

#1—What are your expectations for group interactions among team members?

Team members who do not work well together are a reflection of their leadership. Leaders who permit backbiting and the development of cliques are asking for trouble, both literally and figuratively.

Here's what you need to do:

Set High standards for mutual support, data sharing, effortful cross-training, and learning. *We're in this together.*

- **Mutual Support** There's a place for emotional support when things fall apart. Teams who tear apart other team members when things go wrong only build a fear of failure. *Fear of failure stifles team power and reduces effectiveness.*

- **Data Sharing** is an indication that people are willing to help others in the pursuit of a larger goal. Data hoarding is evidence that someone on the team wants to make themselves more important than others. Leaders, address this issue head on.

- **Effortful Cross-Training** is the apex of team membership. When people are learning from the knowledge others have attained through time, there is a development of mutual respect that strengthens teams. Admiration of one's co-workers is a powerful way to bond team members together.

#2—How well does your team work with other teams in your organization?

In other words, does your team provide mutual support to other groups? Are you willing to share data, resources and time? Is it easy for other teams to work with your team? Do other teams struggle to access your team? *What reputation is your team building for cooperation and collaboration?*

Here's what you need to do:

Set an expectation that the "Silo Mentality" is not workable. Demonstrate that your team is going to help the entire organization achieve the strategies and goals so everyone wins.

How do these two things happen? Leaders model both team interactions and organizational interactions. Your team is watching you. What are you teaching them about group interaction and interactions between groups? Team leadership falls squarely on your shoulders.

How Leaders Create
the Conditions for Motivation

We consistently hear the phrase: "Leaders motivate people." At the risk of organizational heresy, I disagree. Leaders don't motivate anyone: they create the conditions where motivation will arise. Let me explain.

I have listened to many, many people talk about "employee engagement;" the notion that people will expend extra effort in organizational causes. When asked to describe what makes them "engaged," they will say things like:

- *I feel engaged when my opinion matters, and I am heard.*

- *I feel engaged when my leader seeks my advice, and I am respected.*

- *I feel engaged when I am appreciated, and when my leader trusts me.*

If we want to be effective leaders, however, we need to step back and realize that the things people say about engagement reflect the fact that leaders create the conditions for motivation, but do not create motivation itself.

Motivations that are common to all People (*With acknowledgement to the giants: White, and Deci & Ryan, recently made popular by Daniel Pink in DRIVE*):

Effectance Motivation The sense that I am making a difference and creating outcomes.

Competence Motivation The sense that I have the skill and ability to accomplish tasks.

Autonomy Motivation The sense that I am free to influence things that affect my life.

Relatedness Motivation The sense of well-being I attain by being with people I like, and who like me.

So think about that for a moment: Does any leader *really* have access to those powerful internal motivations? No. The only one who has access is the person; the motivation belongs to them. The fusion reactors of internal motivation are at the disposal of the one who owns the reactor.

Yes, people can be *forced* to be competent; to make a difference, but at a much lower level of performance than when freely chosen. Motivation is powerful, but also very delicate. A leadership misstep can create more chaos than construction. We cannot expect to simply draw motivation out of people as if it were something leaders turn off and on.

Leaders understand that no amount of speaking or PowerPoints or morale-boosting posters will ever create motivation. They know they must create the conditions for natural human motivation to arise.

Here are seven specific ways leaders can create the conditions for motivation to arise in each of the motivational domains. These are recommendations from managers who know their stuff.

Effectance Motivation – *I am making a difference*
1. Consistently provide timely feedback on employee results.
2. Communicate the purpose and goals of employee roles.
3. Share data with employees to show them how they're doing.
4. Provide legitimate rewards for a job well done.
5. Let employees critique process.
6. Give them an opportunity to share in planning processes.
7. Acknowledge best practices.

Competence Motivation – *I am good at what I do*

1. Plan to address all learning styles.
2. Train to specific needs in projects.
3. Mentor and share your knowledge.
4. Make clear the idea that there are "no stupid questions" – learning trumps winning.
5. Job rotations that make sense.
6. Ensure understanding of new information.
7. Provide clarity of organizational structures.

Autonomy Motivation – *I have freedom to influence*

1. Demonstrate trust–don't micromanage.
2. Ask, then listen.
3. Provide guidelines, then get out of the way.
4. Provide structure in decision-making, but leave the details to followers.
5. Be flexible.
6. Keep team members involved in the process.
7. Provide active communication that helps people make good decisions.

Relatedness Motivation – *I like these people and they like me*

1. Share success as a team.
2. Share best practices.
3. Plan social outings. (*I once had a team outing teaching baseball to a group of IT engineers from India—what fun watching the cricket players attempting to learn American baseball! We had a blast, and we bonded.*)
4. Use the entire team on big projects.
5. Make room for people to laugh.
6. Work with other leaders to create cross-departmental engagement.
7. Conduct one-on-ones with leader to develop professional rapport.

Make way for motivation, then get out of the way.

Leaders create the conditions for natural human motivation to arise through careful, thoughtful, intentional, and deliberate actions. Leaders use their own motivation to draw out the motivation of others.

The Simple, Yet Difficult, Discipline of Follow-Up

Ever wonder why so many programs, ideas, efforts, thoughts, concepts, and projects come to nothing in your organization? With all the great ideas out there, and all the great innovation happening in companies, why do many initiatives never truly become part of your organization? I conducted an experiment one time with 18 groups of people; 9 got the "treatment," the other 9 did not. What's the treatment?

Follow-up. Pure and simple.

Here's what happened. All of these teams got together to observe a bunch of best practices (another topic for another time). They studied the best practices, learned *about* the best practices, developed plans for implementing the best practices ... *but!*

Only 9 of the teams showed improvement, but they showed *dramatic* improvement over their non-performing peers.

How did we do that?

We got together every 30 days and simply asked, "Have you done what you said you were going to do?" Sounds easy, right? How hard could it be to follow-up on an idea or project? Candidly, it's very hard for several reasons.

Why doesn't follow-up take place? The novelty of a new project wears off as soon as the gravity of the challenge sets in:

Boredom Executives move on to new projects.

Distraction The "shiny new object" syndrome sets in.

Too Busy Workloads are increasing at an ever demanding rate, allowing precious little time to schedule yet another meeting to follow-up.

Ignore It Some folks would prefer to let a sleeping dog lie. If they don't follow-up or remind others, the issue or initiative will simply die a natural, corporate death.

Avoid It Some folks *intentionally* want a project to fade away, because it is drawing too much attention to their failures.

It's hard For most of us, it's simply a lack of discipline.

Anxiety Added workload creates fear that we might fail.

Yet follow-up to anything is the discipline that makes things happen, so what do we need to do?
Simply add a logical follow-up date immediately after a series of decisions are completed: End of the day for the extremely urgent, and end of the week for the rest. For most projects, a 15 or 30 day follow-up is normal.

Invite the same people immediately after your decision and action meeting. Let me stress: *immediately!* You have their attention, and they know why the meeting is needed. Also, ensure their boss is in attendance, and get their bosses' boss, if possible, because accountability drives action—like it or not.

Getting things done requires the simple, but difficult, discipline of follow-up. Your discipline with follow-up will make you successful, because you will get things done.

Your Conference Calls
are Not About You

It's no secret that conference calls are part of our business DNA. While the ability to get a few, or scores, or hundreds (even thousands) of people on one call is a wonderful and efficient communication tool; however, they pose one very serious risk:

The conference call is not about you, it's about your hearers.

Neglecting this important fact causes those hundreds of people to fade quickly into the "land of distraction." One reason this happens is because conference call leaders think they need to fill an entire hour with their own voice. For the listener, the effect is selective listening—at best.

People can always slow you down, but they find it difficult to speed you up.

Let me explain - if you drone on endlessly, without interruption, assuming your audience is paying attention, you're in danger of decelerating your career.

People are *radically* busy. They don't have time for endless droning—they are already on too many conference calls! The fact is, you are not that important, and they are distracted by Google, Yahoo, pictures of their grandkids, etc.

Create a space for dialogue

Speak quickly, clearly, and ask for questions. Establish a bit of dialogue at the beginning of the call to set the stage for discussion. When you ask a question, count to ten *(not out loud, of course!)* to demonstrate listening behavior. The silence is tough on most of us, but we can gain comfort with the space. I have found that people will begin to discover that their com-ments are welcome on calls, but they need to know the "space" is there allowing them to speak. If we trample over their words, we'll get hostile compliance from everyone else.

When we understand that our listeners are the purpose for the call, we will focus on them, because no matter how wonderful our material, slides, pictures, presentations—if our listeners haven't absorbed the material, it was a waste of their time—and yours.

Make every conference call so efficient that people will look forward to what you have to offer *them* because, in the end, its not about you.

How to Waste Your Investment in Team Building

So, you browsed the catalogues for team building exercises, found an "exotic" location for a team building session, booked the flights, booked the hotel rooms, paid for the catering, brought your team together, took pictures of all the goofy, crazy and unusual activity you shared, and then... *you, and everyone else on the team, forgot all about it a few days later.*

You wasted your investment.

Here's why: Team Building exercises only have value *if* they are integrated into the fabric of the organization going forward; improving working relationships and outcomes through efficiencies and accelerated data sharing.

Before you invest in a team building exercise consider the following:

Will this investment *truly* build your team? Too often, managers let HR leaders select the exercises their teams will participate in, without considering the immediate and long-term impact! Managers cannot delegate this responsibility to HR. They need to understand the goals and impacts of the exercises.

How will you strategically assign people into groups where they will most benefit from the experiences and insights gathered through the stress of the exercise? Most importantly, what will you do every week, every month, and every future meeting until you know—with certainty—that the investment of time, effort, energy *(embarrassment, for some),* and dollars *will truly change your organization?*

I am not averse to team building exercises—I spent a portion of my career in HR/OD using those exercises to help teams. Yet, I believe it is critical that managers use every bit of the investment in a way that changes the behavior of the team for the good of the organization; otherwise, it's just a waste of time, money, and human effort that often leads to employee cynicism—*the opposite of team building*. Spend wisely.

SECTION II
TEAM LEADERSHIP
Tools, Techniques & Hot Spots

TECHNIQUES

The Power of Managerial Pictures

Let me guess: The first thing that came to mind was some wild party or a Facebook post that incriminates some individual in a fraudulent or unprofessional activity? I have good news: This chapter has nothing to do with that at all.

Have you ever noticed that people in meetings sometimes have no idea what other people are trying to communicate? For example, in conversations about web reporting you may hear someone say, "We're going to do web reporting for all the regions." Someone else at the table says, "I don't think that's true—Bill says we're doing web reporting by national accounts." Yet another person says, "I heard we're not doing web reporting because no one could make the business case."

Now, many people would just leave the conversation and walk away. The strong executive or leader needs a tool to help people come together and work out the "truth" about the situation.

Without a focus, people invariably get frustrated with each other and, consequently, they get disillusioned with the discussion. It simply seems too complicated to sort out. People are symbolically stumbling all over each other, and you can't figure out why?

What you start with is unlikely what you'll end with, but the picture you put together allows for multiple minds to share a common experience.

Listening for weird quirks on an issue is the first step to assess that something is wrong. If it sounds like multiple viewpoints exist, they probably do. When this starts to happen, I have a suggestion: Draw a picture or, at minimum, write down what you think you've heard. Then, let others weigh in on the picture.

A picture *is* worth a thousand words

Cliche? Folk wisdom? Proverb? Whatever you think it is, the lesson is powerful—especially in complex organizational situations.

What is the benefit? The benefit of a picture is immense. People who use this skill can get multiple points of view together in one room, work out an understanding of the problem, and develop resolutions to move forward. A picture helps negate what is *not* true about the situation.

People can only carry so much in their minds (the standard answer is "seven things"), and many organizational problems have myriad issues to address. Pictures help.

Getting teams to mentally calibrate around a difficult issue is a complex cognitive skill. It is almost intuitive; it takes a sense of "sensing" when things have gone wrong, and a need to get things back on track. A picture is a starting point for resolution that helps minds to connect the dots and to calibrate together.

But what if I can't draw a picture?

Someone on your team, or someone in the meeting, can draw a picture—it doesn't need to be you.

And what if it's not perfect?

All the better. What you start with is unlikely what you'll end with, but the picture you put together allows for multiple minds to share a common experience—that's a big thing in management. Alignment is easy to talk about, but hard to achieve. Pictures help.

From Tales of Woe to Shouts of Victory: Fixing a Broken Team

I sat down with each of the employees on the team I had been assigned to. One by one, they shared their tales of woe: "We can't get any support from anyone!" she said, hysterical. "Why won't these people listen to us?" he screamed, angrily. "I can't get parts for my customer," came another retort.

That was my introduction to management, many years ago. I was hired to supervise a call center and tech support operation. They were the most beat up group of people I had met in business. Three years later, that team won the highest award in the company where we worked.

Every manager and leader has had to face, at one time or another, a promotion into a broken team. Each of us as managers is sometimes faced with the challenge of mending a group of people who are exhausted, downtrodden, and just plain dejected. Teams fall apart for many reasons: disparaging comments about their effectiveness, ineffective team members, excessive management turnover, unclear mission, and failure. The risky part of these teams is they become self-fulfilling prophecies, because poor team chemistry leads to poor team performance, which leads to blaming, which leads to a death spiral of ineffective performance, and on and on.

When we are called into a conference room and told we'll be moving into "X" team, we sometimes hold our breath, knowing the risks involved with managing a broken team. Things can go wrong. There is no question that rebuilding a team's reputation takes time and deliberate effort. This chapter offers several actions you can take to retool and rebuild. Team repair doesn't often fit a linear change path, but teams do respond to deliberate, thoughtful and persistent leadership.

Leading a team to Victory

Lead with confidence, not with your ego.

In the midst of crisis and ongoing poor performance, when the new leader comes in, everyone is skeptical. They've seen all the high priced help come and go, and they're still here, but they still want to believe that someone can help them. Take courage. This is not going to be easy, but dig in and plan for their success, not yours. People are always curious about someone who really wants them to be successful, and is willing to sacrifice ego, position and status to ensure they're successful. Humility is always a safer starting point, by the way, since you don't have nearly so far to fall.

Build trust.

You'll feel weird the first few days on the team. You won't have enough information to make a good decision. You won't know all the nuances of the jobs people do. You'll feel a bit shallow in your responses, but you can still win the day. Authentic talk is the source of trust. People will want to know if their jobs are safe, and if they can trust your word. Those first few weeks are critical. If you don't know an answer, say so. People know when you're bluffing.

Find out what are people really concerned about.

When you sit down to listen to individual members, common themes will emerge. I have found most often that people are looking for the very thing that they can't get while they are under-performing: they want respect. When a team is in turmoil, they often produce less and complain more. The first thing you need to do is assure them that things can be changed, but it's going to take work, and probably some approaches they haven't used before. An honest appraisal of the situation is critical before you make promises of what will change. Your response to the team (after some serious listening): "To build a reputation (and ultimately, to gain respect), our team needs to demonstrate results in a way that is clear to the organization." Oftentimes, people can only see their local situation, and the needs of an executive to clearly see resource loading is not their concern.

State the not-so-obvious.
The most fundamental observation you may make is *that they are a team*. They may never have even thought that way before. Most people are in "departments." Identifying them as a team, even if it is in name to start, puts a different viewpoint on the situation. People on a team are responsible for the success of the team, not just themselves.

Find the naysayers and bring them to your point of view, or neutralize them.
Every team has a ringleader that people look to when confirming or disconfirming a new boss. In one of my situations, I got on a plane and flew to meet the guy who had the most influence on the group. I wanted to hear him out. The very fact that I went to him spoke volumes. In another situation, I listened to a chronic complainer for about 30 minutes, then asked him what he would do to fix things. The greatest fun I ever had was with some naysayers who regularly told me how much stress they were under. At the same time, I contracted a serious illness that caused me to be taken out of the building in an ambulance. When I returned, I faxed the ambulance bill to the team and never heard about stress again. A little dramatic, I know, but it got the message across in a humorous way.

Set the context—where do people fit into the company?
Most people have no idea even why they come to work. They're unclear about their place in the world. Bring some clarity and certainty to that angle of their thought process. Be deliberate about why they matter! What is the context of their life? Why does their work matter? You have to sort that out in a simple, yet clear, way that resonates with people. They won't buy a sales pitch, but they'll believe someone who can make a strong case for why they exist. Here's where we fit into the broader scope of the organization.

Set the vision—where the team can go?

Here's where we can go. Here's what we can do. When setting vision, people will seek something that is credible, yet beyond what they have today. They'll want to know some of the "how will we do that?" answers. Let them know they will be involved in the solution.

Let them know what you've done in the past (with a bit of humility!).

People need to know you're the real thing. They need to see legitimacy. Selling them on a few things you've done is a good starting point. It develops what I call "listening confidence." In other words, they're confident enough in your abilities that they will at least listen.

Set an expectation for excellence.

I once had to explain how a team was perceived by the rest of the organization. It was tough news to bring, but it set the table for high expectations. They knew it was true, but someone had to bring it to the surface. After about two or three weeks into the role, set the course and expectations. You've listened to them. You know enough about the team now. When you hear: "You have no idea how hard this job is!" you'll be able to say, "Well I think I do." You can speak with authority about what you've learned.

Help solve chronic problems—people must see evidence of leadership.

As you've listened to the team members, you've picked up on some chronic problems that have been around forever; if it's a worthy issue, make it your business to fix one of those problems. For me, it was two major things: "We can't get parts," and "We can't work with our co-workers abroad." The solutions were radically different: one required pure data, the other required finesse involving a different culture.

Put them on the map.

After the team scores a few real points, let the world know.

Nothing pumps up a team that was downtrodden like recognition from others that things are moving and changing in a positive direction. One of the mythologies of the corporate world is a fear that recognition will lead to poor performance. The research (and my own experience) shows this is not true. People are proud to work in a group with achievements. Clearly, the manager must be careful to only recognize *"the real thing,"* but if someone on the team has done well, speak loudly. If the whole team has done well, shout it from the rooftops!

Organizations don't know what they don't know. As a leader, you're the one who has to brag about your team. There is a peripheral but powerful motivational benefit: no one wants to go backward. Once the team has shown what it can do, the bar is set and your expectations can be pushed even higher. People like being part of a win, and they will hold their position at all costs.

Recognition and legitimate validation.
When people know they're valued for their legitimate accomplishments, and they know the organization acknowledges what they've done, meaning has been added to their lives. Think about it: most people will spend their entire work lives wondering if they mattered. You can change that, if only for a moment.

Improve Your Leadership Skills: Manage Volunteers

Organizational Citizenship Behavior is the theory which states that, given the right circumstances and leadership, people will go above and beyond their daily expected work to do more on behalf of the corporation. In a way, they are "volunteering" for additional workload.

D.W. Organ defined organizational citizenship behaviors as "individual behavior that is discretionary, not directly or explicitly recognized by the formal reward system, and that in the aggregate promotes the effective functioning of the organization. By discretionary, we mean that the behavior is not an enforceable requirement of the role or the job description, that is, the clearly specifiable terms of the person's employment contract with the organization; the behavior is rather a matter of personal choice, such that its omission is not generally understood as punishable."

Volunteer comes from the Latin, *Voluntārius,* meaning willingness or inclination. Volunteers willingly do things that others may not want to do. Volunteers apply effort *without pay*, simply because of their own internal focus on the goal, or task, or cause. They are going out of their way to add their energy to help.

I recall more than one conversation where I heard phrases like: *"We don't need to recognize people, because that's what they get paid to do,"* or, *"That's your job."* Whether we all want to admit it or not, that ethos is a prevailing culture in many companies, and it is reasonable, because people do get paid for what they do; however, that managerial style is not likely to get us a whole lot more effort when we need it. If you've volunteered to help in some way, think about this chapter in the context of your experience.

Given the concept of Organizational Citizenship Theory, I often wonder why volunteers do a better job in their work than some paid staff. Clearly there is a difference in the way managers must treat volunteers: managers treat volunteers a bit differently, because they *have to*.

- Managers show a little more respect when they're asking volunteers for help.
- Managers have a greater sensitivity to volunteer efforts when adding to their workload.
- Managers have a stronger awareness of the demands on volunteer time.

Volunteers expect to be treated a bit differently, because their work is *above and beyond* normal life. Consider the following:

- They won't work for someone they don't trust.
- They know their skills matter.
- They know they're adding value.
- They know you need their help.
- They can "walk" at any time without warning.
- They won't work for a cause they don't believe in.
- They want to use their time wisely.
- They want to ensure they know their role.
- They want to know if you're serious about the project!

Think about those behaviors for a minute, then think another minute. How much additional effort does it take to manage people who have the expectations of volunteers? From what I can see, the expectations of employees and the expectations of volunteers are only different in the element of compensation.

All employees want to trust their leaders. Most employees know their skills matter and that they add value by their presence. Employees know you need their help—after all, that's why you hired them in the first place. Although it's a bit tough to find another job, employees have the prerogative to "walk" at any time without warning. They want to work for causes they believe in, and they want to use their time in their role wisely. And, in the end, they'll watch your behavior to see if you're invested, or merely marking time.

A slight re-framing can help us be better Leaders.

We treat our guests better than our families, and we treat customers better than our staff. A slight re-framing of our managerial attitudes toward workers, as if they were volunteers, may be a bit extreme but, in the end, the willingness of staff to go the extra mile, *to strain beyond their normal duties,* is likely a factor of whether we treat them like laborers or people who are going out of their way to help.

SECTION II
TEAM LEADERSHIP
Tools, Techniques & Hot Spots

HOT SPOTS

"We're Done Here:"
Managing the Hard Cases

Much leadership literature is dedicated to visioning, innovation, production and achievement, yet little is said about the tough stuff. In this way, business imitates life. Few of us want bad news, fewer still want to admit there is a problem, and fewer still want to deal with conflict. And yet, leading people invariably raises the issues of "hard cases;" those team members who raise havoc that requires the intervention of termination.

Clearly, the first person to examine is you! Is there something in your leadership style that is generating negative reactions or unwanted resistance? Sometimes, leaders create their own problems through ineffective management, but I'm not speaking directly to that issue in this chapter. I'm focused exclusively on the belligerent, the recalcitrant, the incompetent, and the repugnant.

Those who create drama *whenever there is a change.*

In my experience, there is a large group who initially react negativity to change but, over time, with some coaching and a good rationale, most people will come around. Yet there are those who simply want to create a Federal case out of new changes, and they will spend excessive amounts of time explaining why the change will *never* work. They create unnecessary barriers and invent rumors to derail necessary programs. In my opinion, this draws attention to them, but perhaps not in a way they expect. I have seen this type of person change if you point out the issue.

The response is straightforward: "This train has left the station. You have a choice to be on board, or not on board, but that choice is yours."

Those who refuse to cooperate—those who *will not.*

There are those who, under no circumstances, will cooperate with your vision or your approach. You have listened to them, and you've carefully heard them out, but they will not accept the path you're on. In those situations, I've often discovered something much bigger is at work. While I'm not a psychologist, I do believe issues of resentment for losing a valued role in the organization may be at the bottom of some of those circumstances. As a leader, you simply cannot correct the past! When employees are punishing you to exact revenge for a misdeed long ago, the only thing you can do is remove them.

The response is straightforward: "We've had our discussions many times. I've listened, but we both know this is not going to work. "

Those who are unable—those who *cannot.*

We sometimes inherit team members from other departments during major organizational shifts. When that happens, we soon discover some people who simply cannot do the job. Good leaders and managers take the time to build skills and help people out, but the best leaders discover when a person simply is not going to make it.

The response is straightforward: "We've tried, and you've made some effort, but this role is beyond your skill level; you know it and I know it. Let's make a plan for your exit."

Those who *damage team morale.*

This type of employee has, arguably, the worst impact of them all. There is psychological research that demonstrates "one bad apple can spoil the whole bunch." This employee has gone beyond publicly disagreeing with you—they are determined to prevent the team from being successful and, in the end, they want to "bring you down."

The response is straightforward: "You're a talented, gifted individual, but you've chosen to use those abilities to damage the lives of others. You need to move on."

The benefits to managing the hard cases:
Of course you'll need clear documentation to terminate some-one, and you must follow good HR practice with a strong HR partner, but in the end:

- Your team will thank you.
- You will gain leadership credibility (because no one wants to do the hard stuff, but you did!).
- Your team morale will improve.
- Your team productivity will improve.
- You'll probably sleep better at night.
- Your own level of self-respect will grow a hundred-fold.

How to Tell if Your Leadership Team Acts Like a Rock Band

Rock musicians are a special breed. They have to be, for the initial stages of rock and roll stardom are anything but glamorous. The experience of facing awful crowds, overcoming terrible venues, poor sound, bad electrical outlets, traveling through terrible snow storms, having little or no lighting, awful management, and playing in the hot sun for hours just to get a few dollars (or whatever denomination fits their nation) is the introduction to the rock scene. It ain't pretty, but for those who persist, it builds efficacy and, before long, the energy, excitement, and glory of performing before a live audience becomes it's own allure.

Executive teams are also a special breed. They work long, tortuous hours to get to the top, often facing (and surviving) horrendous bosses along the way. They, too, develop efficacy in their roles, and they feel the allure of power that comes through influence. They take dramatic risks, and often they spend more time at their jobs than doctors because, for many, the roles are 24/7/365.

The two groups have some striking similarities:
We call the best performers what? "Rock Stars!" High levels of investment in time and energy are required to get recognized in both domains. To get to the top requires *years* of practice, discipline, and pain.

You might have a leadership team that acts like a rock band if:

- The level of talent does not match the intensity of the ego.
- The lure of organizational applause blinds leaders to their

own mediocre performance.

- Self-importance is raised to the level of narcissism. Artists are very self-focused–their creativity is their own subjective world, and they believe it's important for others to listen to them. Garage bands may feel like they're very good, but they often need a reality check. Ego happens in business too, sometimes to the detriment of many.
- When everyone wants to do something *different*. Rock bands are notorious for arguing for hours about "what kind of music are we going to play?" Ever seen an executive team endlessly argue about a strategic plan?
- When there's lots of *air guitar* (people flailing their arms and making gestures without truly producing music). In business, we sometimes call this Power Point.
- Excessive amplification (When the voice gets louder, and louder, and louder!). Amplification serves to bring attention to the performer, and this happens in business, as well. When everyone wants to talk louder and gain greater attention, executives are acting like rock bands. Power is intoxicating! Sometimes, the temptations of power exceed self-restraint.
- Some band members may not be "all there," and some leaders should not be in their roles.
- Perks and Special Parking are expectations irrespective of performance.
- Leadership discussions wander all without focus like *the Dreaded Band Meeting* ...

The best bands have focus:
The Rolling Stones have been around for over 50 years because they focus, and they continually work together on a singular sound, but they are the rare exception! Does your leadership team have focus??

The best bands listen to each other:
This may sound strange to the non-musician, but "listening to each other" creates the space for collaboration in music: one takes the lead, then another, working together in—yes—

harmony!

The best bands use the skills of every member to create an overall sound:
When all the parts of a rock band are working together, the outcome borderlines on magic. People become energized, enthusiastic, and find joy in their lives under the influence of a great sound where all the parts fit together. In business, teams that function with maximum effectiveness are using every person for the benefit of all.

How did I gain this special insight? I spent years in rock bands *and* in business! I've seen both worlds up close, and the similarities are rather intriguing, *don't you think?*

Beware This Corporate Guilt Trip:
"You're Not a Team Player"

For all who work in the Corporate world, there comes a day when we're in a critical meeting, and someone very powerful points to us and uses this phrase: **you're not a team player.**

While it is never wise to question the motives of others, it is safe (and fair) to consider the impact of the phrase, since it may be one of the most manipulative string of words in the English language. Here are some of the implications:

- *You're obviously not willing to help us all succeed.*
- *You're obviously in this for your own gain.*
- *You're not thinking of the bigger picture.*
- *You're not interested in our success.*

It is a crushing phrase that immediately puts us on the defensive. As soon as that happens, we're on the ropes, and with a flushed face of embarrassment, we begin explaining that we are indeed willing to help; willing to be part of something; willing to see the team succeed. (Meanwhile, *at the back of our minds, we know we don't have the resources, span of control, time, funding, and extra hands to complete the task we've been challenged with.*)

Those who use the phrase know exactly what they're doing. They are putting people into the uncomfortable place of having to commit to something out of sheer guilt and fear of a loss of reputation. In some cases, I believe it borders on extortion.

If you've been a target of this questionable phrase, consider whether this is a consistent method of the person's managerial tactics. If so, others know, because they've experienced the same tactic. Be diplomatic but direct: "My track record demonstrates a consistently high level of support for this organization, and we'll do what needs to be done, but let me offer that this project stands in the way of several other major corporate initiatives. Just so I'm clear, what's the priority?"

If you've used this questionable phrase, rethink your approach. There are far better ways to gain team member collaboration without resorting to manipulative pressure. Only weak leaders turn to this type of tactic. Over the long run, your reputation will precede you and people will come to expect this sort of behavior. This phrase is sophomoric, at best.

Embarrassing team members into cooperation may work in the short term but, over the long haul, you'll build resentment and lose key people.

End of Section Personal Review

- **Does this Section address a part of your leadership/ management style that you need to improve on?**

Notes_____

_____

_____

_____

- **Do you need to share a chapter in this book with a colleague?**

Notes_____

_____

_____

_____

- **Does this Section address an issue that relates to your workplace?**

Notes_____

_____

_____

_____

- **Is there advice in this Section that would be helpful to implement in your workplace?**

Notes_____

_____

_____

_____

SECTION III

ORGANIZATIONAL LEADERSHIP
Tools, Techniques & Hot Spots

TOOLS

Your Organization is Unique, but Your Leadership Problems are the Same

As a social scientist who has worked with many of the Fortune 500 in my travels, I have had the opportunity to observe organizational patterns repeated over and over again. Having some global experience, I am also confident these issues transcend geography. Whether a company makes paper products, produces allergy medication, provides telecom service to millions, or draws crude oil from the earth, all organizations have one thing in common: their leadership issues are the same. This chapter describes four leadership issues that are common to all organizations: *Organizational Attention Deficit Disorder*, *Siloing*, *Ineffective Managers*, and *Mediocre Organizational Communications*.

The common goal:
People working together in organizations.

At the end of the day, the defining element of organizational behavior is this: *are people working together to accomplish significant and critical corporate goals?* Leaders are responsible to make that happen! So what are the common leadership challenges among organizations?

Organizational Attention Deficit Disorder
Organizational Attention Deficit Disorder is an organization's inability to focus on the critical few, accepting any and all projects as worthy of priority effort, resulting in employee burnout and organizational ineffectiveness. This trend is increasing, and calls for organizational simplification. Here are the sources of O.A.D.D.:

- The development and distribution of policies, programs, processes and practices from any and all teams without a coordinative center causes confusion among middle managers trying to implement everything that is sent to them.

- The immense amount of change happening in any organization at one time is a major source of OADD.
- Management changes cause disruption, since people are uncertain about what priorities will matter to a new leader.
- Organizational restructuring causes disruption, since people will focus on their *next job* rather than the work at hand.
- Executive teams are sometimes "at odds" with one another, creating uncertainty in the ranks. People wonder "who will come out on top" in a organizational battle for dominance *(yes, it happens!),* and thus play a "wait-and-see" game, causing OADD.

Over the long haul, employees and team members learn how their leadership manages (*or does not manage*) OADD. Organizations will always be distracted by something (a new technology, a new Federal requirement, a new competitor, a new product), but focusing employees on the critical few sets a stage for achievement and success. Team members want to know that their hard work will result in achievement of the goal. ***This is a chronic leadership issue that must be addressed to improve organizational performance.***

Organizational Siloing

I shall never forget the experience I had with two people from different departments, one floor apart in the same building, who had never met each other! Two groups (Engineering and Procurement) existed in the same building for decades. When I raised an issue that required them to be together to solve an issue, I heard one of them say, "*I had no idea you were in this building.*"

This sort of thing is indicative of groups that rarely venture out into the rarefied air of other groups unless they absolutely have to. Organizational siloing is a serious matter in organizations because it impedes collaboration and effective solutions. *This is a chronic leadership issue that must be addressed to improve organizational performance.*

Managerial Ineffectiveness

Statistics vary on the percentage of ineffective managers in organizations, but some estimates I have read set the number as high as 70%. Although people may have managerial jobs and formally assigned roles, they may not be at all effective at leading teams or developing employees. They remain in positions of power that affect (and sometimes damage!) the lives of others in negative ways, reducing organizational performance. They are ineffective in the way they hire, the way they coordinate actions, the way they recognize, and the way they evaluate performance. *This is a chronic leadership issue that must be addressed to improve organizational performance.*

Mediocre Organizational Communication

The belief that pressing "send" creates effective communication is a pervasive notion in organizations, even though many people realize it rarely changes people's views or moves things forward. Leaders use sound bites to communicate complex issues due to a lack of patience, and a belief that communication "is going to take hours." Communication is hard work! Communication takes additional effort and time to ensure the message got through. Most organizations I have worked with struggle mightily with this issue, because top leaders believe that communication is going on all the time, simply because people talk to each other. *This is a chronic leadership issue that must be addressed to improve organizational performance.*

I have a good friend who has been a social worker for over 40 years. He said this to me: "Dysfunction in business is due to dysfunctional people." My corollary to that is this: "Dysfunction in business is due to dysfunctional leadership practices."

If leaders cannot focus people toward a goal and remove distractions; if they continue to support a silo culture which separates people; if they retain (or do not retrain) bad managers who damage good employees; and, if they cannot overcome ineffective communications through deliberate effort, their organizations will suffer. Great leaders, however, see these patterns, and address them to achieve marvelous results.

The Critical Element of Leading Organizational Changes

I recently led a roundtable discussion with executives from companies that provide services ranging from pharmacy to high tech, and from security to transportation. The topic was change management, a hot button for all involved. Changes ranged from introduction of new IT systems to policy changes, and from mergers and acquisitions to wholesale transformation and global standardization of services. The energy in the conversation built around one major theme: the psychological elements of change are essential for change adoption.

"Where's the empathy in an e-mail?"

Members of the roundtable lamented the lack of effectiveness in much change communication. While e-mail is effective for mass communication, it does not build the trust necessary for change adoption. E-mail communication alone is a distant and cold method for helping people adjust to change. Simply put: people want to know that the person initiating the change isn't simply pushing the "send" button, but actually *cares* about the impact on their lives. Trust is the critical element.

Up close and personal is the way to build trust and reduce fear. Everyone at the table said they felt the best way to communicate change was through face-to-face communication. They talked about non-verbal nuances and the ability to access a person's concerns through facial expressions and even seating arrangements. In other words, it's good to talk. While the notion of face-to-face seems impossible with massive changes, the attendees acknowledged there is always a way to get to the front lines to explain the change. Fear dissipates when people can see each other and recognize the truth in statements.

Honesty and trust remain key elements in the adoption of change. The wariness that comes with the introduction of new things can be overcome by honest acknowledgement of people's concerns, and by truthful descriptions of the "why, what, and how?" of the change. Hidden agendas, deceptive communications, and cryptic messaging are ineffective in developing the relationships necessary for change adoption.

The stronger the personal relationships, the easier the adoption. "How are the kids?" was one of the questions a roundtable participant used as an example of building relationships. What he was demonstrating was simply this: when people know you're interested in their lives, at least at some emotional level, they're far more inclined to believe you have their best interest at heart during a change.

No one believes "corporate," but they will believe their peers. Many participants talked of the need to engage peers in the discussion and implementation of the change. Peers are in the trenches, struggling with the same issues every day, so they understand the problems of others facing the change. This is especially critical during changes that affected multiple cultures—people need to be heard and understood in their own language, idioms, culture and phraseology.

The heart of the matter? The emotional part of change is not going away. People will not easily adjust to imposed change without a sense that those leading the change are willing to develop the trust, display honesty, and demonstrate concern for those affected by change. Those managers and leaders who take these things to heart will be successful in the initiatives they undertake, because people will believe they have their best interests in mind.

Effective Recognition: The Cure for Organizational Malaise

At a recent speaking engagement, I heard it again. "Recognition will lead to a slow down in employee effort." That sort of comment contributes to organizational malaise, a sense employees get that they're just putting in time for a company that has little concern about them as people.

This mythology is pervasive in today's organizations. It's astonishing to me because Millennials now make up the largest part of the workforce, and it seems they would be leading the charge on effective recognition. Millenials are ostensibly more enlightened than their Boomer counterparts, so we would expect more interest in employee recognition.

Here are some of the mythologies I've heard about recognition through the years:

- *If you reward people, they'll stop working.*
- *They get a paycheck—they should be happy with that.*
- *It takes extra effort to do this sort of thing.*
- *They'll come to expect extra stuff.*
- *We shouldn't recognize bad performance.*

There are other variations of these phrases, but you get the picture. Looking at the concerns in total, you get the idea that any extra thanks or recognition will bring things to a halt. Candidly, a lack of recognition contributes to organizational malaise; that feeling you get when you're just not sure if your work matters at all.

You give the basics, you get the basics.

Let's think about this for just a moment. Yes, the unwritten social contract states: "If you do this amount of work, I'll pay you $xyz." Agreed. That's fundamental, but if that is where leaders stop, their effectiveness is sorely limited. *Everyone* gets a paycheck, but not everyone performs to maximum capacity. There are many who simply do "collect the paycheck;" that's all they've ever expected from their employers, because they've never seen anything beyond the basics.

Recognition taps far deeper motivational resources than a simple paycheck.

People work their whole lives and wonder, "Did I matter?" Recognition validates people by showing them that their efforts matter, and by showing them that their lives matter. To be valued as a human being is at the root of much psycho-therapeutic and spiritual literature. Ever wonder why? Because people need to know if their lives mattered at all.

I have seen people who were downtrodden, beat up, and rejected by their organizations come alive as recognition was *effectively* used to bring them out of their depression—because, in the end, that's what it is.

You don't need to spend a million dollars to recognize someone, but your organization does want people to bring their best, to improve, to achieve, to accomplish great things. *Intrinsic motivation is the key to achievement.* The research bears that out. Tapping intrinsic motivation goes well beyond money. Intrinsic motivation is about achievement and success, not just a paycheck. I tell people all the time, "Do not underestimate the motivational power of $50 worth of pizza for a job well done—especially as the hard work continues."

Interestingly, a big splash of money rarely gets the long-term effect you're looking for. You'll argue, "That's not true—look how much high level executives get paid!" Ever think about why that money is important to them? So they can satisfy intrinsic motivations including altruism, power, philanthropy and, in some cases, self- justification for overcoming tragedy and major personal challenges. It's not just about the money—it's about the internal satisfaction it brings.

No one recognized me, so I don't need to recognize others.

I've heard this thinly veiled grudge in meetings and among "tough minded" managers. You may not have had recognition, and your corporation may be uncomfortable with the idea, but you and your organization are interested in stellar, high-performing teams. A paycheck will not bring about major achievements, and your long-standing grudge will not help anyone—it just perpetuates the cycle. (*This is the corporate equivalent to the difficulties of getting a Ph.D. "People put me through all kinds of hoops to get my doctorate, so I'm going to return the favor."*) As a leader, get past that personal grudge and help others. It can be very motivating.

Bad performance should not be recognized.

I fully agree. Having good metrics in place really helps when the time comes for recognition.

Sincerity in recognition trumps grandstanding.

The worst possible thing you can do is thank someone in an insincere manner. Better not to thank someone at all, than to act as if you care when you don't. You've just devalued them one more time.

The excuses for not recognizing people are old, tiring, and un-helpful. Be a leader. Thank people. Validate their lives. Build them up. Then watch your team outshine everyone in the cor-poration.

HR's Role in Repairing Reputations

Mary (not her real name, but a true story) had something go wrong during a presentation. There was a lot on the line, and the customer was dissatisfied with the presentation. It cost the corporation a million dollars in potential revenue. Mary had made a mistake and failed. Her mistake became mythology.

Years later, Mary continued to be haunted by the event. Mary was an outstanding employee in every other way, but this one event raised it's ugly head every time Mary's name was mentioned. Mary was sidestepped and ignored during promotional opportunities, and at one time micromanaged to the point of exhaustion. What people did not know at the time was that Mary had significant anxiety about presentations, but had not shared her fears about presenting because of concern for her job. She had spent many years avoiding presentations but could not avoid the one that damaged her career. She needed help to restore her reputation.

Human Resources can help repair damaged reputations

Human Resources can make a radical and helpful difference in the lives of others by managing the truth about situations involving mistakes or failures. There are a few very crisp and legitimate ways to analyze a situation and help a person reclaim their reputation in the midst of failure.

One time failure, or chronic issue? An employee's reputation is his or hers to make—we all agree to that truth. People own their careers and reputations but, in the midst of a failure, people need advocacy from others who can fairly and honestly evaluate whether someone messed up once on a grand scale, or if performance is always substandard (and even then, it's worth assessing the reasons why). Once the truth is made known, people need help recovering lost ground.

Group failure, or individual failure? Did the person in question fail on their own, or were others (including executives) involved in the project? Was it negligence on the part of one, or a lack of coordination and collaboration on the part of many? Was a *post mortem* conducted to assess the true cause of failure? Is it owned by one or many? How much of the issue is owned by leadership of the project?

Fall guy, or scapegoat? Sometimes, people do "take a fall" for others. The question is, does that fall become a valuable sacrifice to leverage later on, or is it simply one manager stepping on another to gain advantage? Is a person a "scapegoat" for the flaws of others? If so, the organization may have a deeper issue than a project failure. HR can take the time to discover the truth.

Seeking truth, not perpetuating Myths

Whilst we all make mistakes in our careers, sometimes there are more nefarious elements at play. Sometimes there is intentional career sabotage, for all the ill-conceived reasons that human nature can devise, including jealousy, envy, and a desire for power. HR can root out those who desire to disparage the reputations of others—it takes courageous truth-seeking and speaking, but it can be done.

HR can restore reputations and, in so doing, maintain employees who have done wonderful work, but perhaps tripped up along the way. While some things are simply inexcusable and grounds for zero-tolerance, most employee errors can be significant learning experiences, and for the determined souls who want to rescue their reputations, HR can be a powerful resource. And, if the person in question has legitimately damaged their reputation, a courageous HR person can make that point very clear so someone can move on.

Why is this important? Humans seek justice; it's a simple fact of life. Unjustly disparaged reputations can damage a person for a long time—maybe even for life. HR can help by creating an atmosphere and culture of truth, not mythology, by debunking mythologies that harm employees and, ultimately, reduce motivational power.

No one works perfectly for their entire career. Sometimes we make mistakes, and then we need help to get up off the ground after failure. HR can do that.

SECTION III
ORGANIZATIONAL LEADERSHIP
Tools, Techniques & Hot Spots

TECHNIQUES

What Makes an Organization Tick?

Why do organizations exist? Ask any leader what they consider as the ultimate goal in their work and, most likely, they'll tell you: "It's about the organization. It's about the survival of the business in the face of competition. It's about winning."

Business is about the effectiveness of the Organization, not the needs of any specific individual—so why do we continue to evaluate at the employee level? This is not a cynical, unfeeling statement that disregards employee concerns. At its root, it is a profound statement of a desire to sustain a business; helping businesses to succeed under mounting local and global pressure, with a desire to continue employment for team members. Organizations need to survive *at the organizational level.*

Yet, the common focus of most organizational improvement today is at the individual level, with its roots in the work of Harter, Schmidt, and others, dating from 1999 to the early 2000's. "Employee Engagement" has been around for over 15 years.

Current Approaches to Organizational Analysis
Studies show that while over 70% of companies conduct employee engagement surveys, less than 30% are satisfied with the results. This has been a constant theme for some time. Executives are interested in improving their organizations, but fail to evaluate the overall level of organizational functioning because the current state of organizational analysis is focused on individual employee responses, not the organizational level.

After four decades of managing teams, workplace involvement and observations, personal engagements with scores of companies, and through academic research, I have observed these **Common (and Chronic) Organizational Problems:**
• Organizations are often siloed. That is, departments focus

on their own needs to the exclusion of the success of others. This behavior has a significant negative impact on organizational output.

- Managers are defocused because of excessive (and sometimes, conflicting) initiatives.
- People are sometimes uncertain about how their work fits into organizational success, exacerbating ineffectiveness.
- Leaders use sound bytes to communicate, often leading to confusion.
- Ineffective projects and programs are left in place, draining precious organizational time and energy.

What does that look like in practice?

- People do not communicate effectively enough to provide data flow and make effective decisions.
- People do not work together to solve problems.
- People are unsure of how they support the organization's mission.
- Incomplete or unnecessary projects absorb valuable resources.
- The organization demonstrates poor levels of managerial accountability.
- Ineffective leaders remain in positions of authority, negatively influencing others.

These are clearly organizational level issues, not employee level issues, yet organizations are most often analyzed from an individual's viewpoint, either through interviews or surveys. Here are a few approaches that have been used within recent decades:

Organizational Culture

First of all, one of the major challenges in organizational analysis is the definition of "culture." It is an oblique word, with as many meanings as there are people in the room. Culture is a glamorous, intriguing word, and it has the sophisticated ring of ... well, culture! The problem is, culture is often vague and difficult to pin down. Deference to culture allows those who do not want to change, the ability to say "it's a cultural issue," providing them an excuse to continue on with their same old practices. (Human Systems Dynamics Institute calls culture "a short hand name for a pattern.")

Culture is "the glue that binds an organization together ... it is the collection of values, beliefs, symbols, and norms the organization follows, and that define what it is and how it does business each and every day (*SHRM, Fornal, 2002*)."

Cultural analyses, while helpful, do not provide solutions to the roots of the culture itself. Let me explain. Foundational researchers would offer this: "Culture is the way we do things around here." *If that's the case, then we need to resolve what it is we're doing and how we're doing it; then make changes that correct the way we do things.* If culture is "the way we do things around here," why not analyze that? Ineffective organizational culture costs thousands, even millions of dollars for organizations every year.

OCAI Instrument

The Organizational Culture Assessment Instrument (*Cameron & Quinn*) emphasizes culture types within different organizations, including Clan Culture, Adhocracy Culture, Market Culture, and Hierarchy Culture. This is a prominent instrument in organizational assessment. The approach is one of looking at the entire organization through a lens that assesses the framework of organizational culture or, in other words, *the way we do things around here.* As with most instruments like this, organizations begin to "see" themselves as they have assessed themselves. *The approach used, however, is that of how the individual employee sees the organization.*

Organization Based Self-Esteem

This measurement is focused on how an individual employee feels about himself or herself in the midst of an organization. In other words, how does participation in a specific organization contribute to one's self-esteem? (*1989 Pierce, Gardner,*

Cummings, and Dunham). Researchers explain: " … signals to employees that they 'make a difference around here' and that that difference is valued by the organization are positively related to this self-concept. Organization-based opportunities for positive and successful experiences were also found to have a positive relationship with OBSE."

This organizational analysis is focused on how the individual responds to the organization's support of their self-esteem, not the organization's ability to produce output.

Organizational Commitment

Organizational commitment has been conceptualized as "an *individual's* attitude towards the organization, consisting of a strong belief in, and acceptance of, an organization's goals, willingness to exert considerable effort on behalf of the organization, and a strong desire to maintain membership in the organization" (*Eby, Freeman, Rush, & Lance, 1999*). The individual's view of the organization is also the lens used in this approach. What is the organization doing *for me* so I may do something to benefit it?

Organizational Climate

Kopelman et al. (1990) wrote, "Climate is the psychological process that mediates the relationships between the work environment (conceived as an objective set of organizational policies, practices and procedures) and work-related attitudes and behaviors". Climate includes the following five things: autonomy, reward, support, participation, and warmth. This is sometimes referred to as "psychological climate." One primary aspect of climate is "socioemotional support," which is "the extent to which employees perceive that their personal welfare is protected by kind, considerate, and generally humane management."

Once again, the individual's view of the organization is the lens used by this approach (and, in my opinion, "climate" sounds a lot like "culture").

Organizational Citizenship

Organizational citizenship behaviors include such things as "helping others with their jobs, volunteering for additional work, and supporting organizational objectives" (*Judge et al., 2001, p. 381, citing Borman & Motowidlo, 1993, and Organ, 1990*). The purpose for measuring this construct is to assess how much additional effort people are willing to expend in pursuit of organizational objectives. Productivity and performance are the primary goals of such instruments and interventions.

Where do the elements of citizenship arise? How is it that people feel so much a part of an organization that they are willing to expend additional effort? A culture that enhances citizenship does not happen at the individual employee level.

Organizational Health

Patrick Lencioni's book, "The Advantage" touts Organizational Health. While it is a significant accomplishment, it doesn't assess how things get done at the organizational level. The focus of the book is primarily on the leadership team and clarity of mission. Yet the overall view of how the organization functions is still not part of the analysis.

Maybe the secret lies in Six Sigma and Lean

For Organizational Transformation to take place, we need specifics, so let's do process mapping, Lean Sigma; let's build scores of projects that increase ROI. Still, we *know* this approach does not solve questions at the organizational level. While we may increase the number of cost saving projects, we still do not understand the bigger issues of what hinders organizational effectiveness.

Perceived Organizational Support

Eisenberger (2011) gets a little closer to an organizational focus: "Management must be constantly on guard to be sure that the bureaucracy of the organization facilitates the basic goals and objectives of the organization rather than interfering with them," but he is still focused on the individual. Perceived Organizational Support is about how the organization supports the *individual*, not the other way around.

(And, returning to the beginning:) Employee Engagement

A prominent method of organizational analysis is employee engagement—how much are employees "engaged" or involved? Established by Gallup's Q12, Employee Engagement remains a key focus for organizational analysis. Yet, the items in the Q12 are all self-focused, not organizationally focused. Thus, the organizational benefits accruing to the individual is the lens used by this approach. *What is the organization doing for me so I may benefit?*

Summary of the approaches:

The individual's view of the organization is the lens used by the majority of organizational analyses, but the big question remains—*what makes an organization tick?* With all the organization development work that has been done through the past several decades, significant and serious fundamental questions still remain.

- What brings together all of the forces of an organization, including people, process, tools, training, and leadership?
- What is happening at the organizational level to bring about the accomplishments, completed projects, and strategic achievements the organization desires?
- What can leaders do at the organizational level to bring together organizational achievements?

Organizational level efficacy is the result of the entire organization in action. Organizational level efficacy is the missing analysis.

Is Your Organizational Behavior Driving People Away?

When we somehow believe that employees are at fault for unresolved organizational issues, we have the problem statement backwards! Employee retention is about more than employee survey engagement tactics. Employee retention is an organizational level issue that can only be managed by effective leadership willing to take steps to improve collective organizational behavior.

We hear a lot about employee retention, but not so much about the sources of employee exits. If we do, there may be some *mea culpa* about 'the wrong manager," or "lack of opportunities," or "he/she wasn't a fit," but I think something far greater is at work, and I am not alone.

A study by Alan Church *(2013)* revealed that a major concern in employee engagement for high potential employees was "My company is effectively managed and well run" *OD Practitioner, (45, 2)*. What does that tell us? High potential employees are concerned about the *overall effectiveness of an organization*, not just the component parts, and yet we're likely to blame standard engagement practices as the source of organizational problems. Here's a quote that describes the "blame game:"

> "At the root of many engagement theories is a kind of wishful thinking that business concerns will resolve themselves if only employees were more engaged."
> *(Brooks and Saltzman, 2012 People and Strategy)*

That means organizational leaders (including HR) place the burden of employee retention squarely on the shoulders of [drum roll] the employees! Not logical, not accurate, not helpful, and surely not effective. The individual employee has little effect on overall engagement and organizational effectiveness. *It is the organizational level that matters.* When organizational level strategies and goals are unclear, people leave.

Effectance Motivation

In 1959, Robert W. White wrote a classic article for Psychological Review titled, *Motivation Reconsidered: The Concept of Competence.* In it, White proposed a new concept: Effectance Motivation. "Effectance" was described as a "tendency to explore and influence the environment." White suggested that the "master reinforcer" for humans is personal competence. He defined competence as "the ability to interact effectively with the environment." White explained that people (he said organisms, but we'll bypass that discussion for now) need to feel a motivational sense of *effectance*; a sense of accomplishing or moving something.

How many times have you heard someone say, "I just want to make a difference." That's the issue at the motivational heart of this problem. Enter poorly designed organizational strategies and management ineffectiveness. People do not have time to waste on ineffectiveness. They want to feel a sense of competence. They want to know they "moved the needle." They want to know their lives mattered!

When employees talk to each other and say "I feel like we're going no where. We have no direction. We don't know what's happening," you have trouble and you're likely to lose people. Retaining employees is a matter of bringing meaning into their lives. Leaders must take stock of whether their organization is driving employees away, and then change the organizational level behavior, especially in a rapidly changing demographic where newer generations are seeking meaning in their lives through work.

I've said it before and I'll say it again: it is the organizational level that matters. Leadership is the answer to the exodus.

Simplifying Organizations:
The Discipline We Must Pursue

The axiom of "Publish or Perish" has held sway in Academe for decades. There are certain things scholars must do to maintain their status in the academic world. The organizational corollary is "Simplify or Perish." Simplicity is a critical element of success that organizations must attend to, to maintain *their* status in the world.

Are you kidding me?

You might say "We have programs to manage, products to produce, people to train, systems to put in place, and policies to practice. How can we possibly simplify all of this effort?" Fair question.

While you may balk at the idea, leaders cannot overlook the importance of reducing complexity within their organizations. Management of complexity requires cognitive effort that is best used in the creation, design and production of real value. Every additional thought, every unnecessary expenditure of energy, every meeting held to address useless trivia, and every management level put in place to attend to dying projects, all contribute to a loss of employee engagement and, ultimately, a loss of revenue and profit.

The Roots of Organizational Complexity
So where does organizational complexity come from? Having worked with many of the Fortune 100 in different capacities, here are the sources I have observed:

- **Leadership Turnover** Frequent turnover of leadership allows unfinished programs to run on unmanaged; continuing to absorb resources. Does anyone even know where some projects started?!

- **People "making their mark"** People attempting to make their mark devise new programs and new routines that aggregate through the years.
- **People holding on to their "mark" (AKA, "faded glory.")** Some folks just want to ensure that their special program continues to get the attention it got thirty years ago when it was valuable and useful to the business. For some managers—even some executives—this is their legacy, and they don't want anyone to tamper with it.
- **Clean up is not all that exciting.** Who wants to take the time to simplify? Who gets rewarded for simplicity?
- **"It's not my job."** We're all busy, and we really don't want to be the one to clean up someone else's mess.
- **"Who's minding the store?"** Where is the Air Traffic Controller who has taken the time to look over the vast array of unattended projects in an organization?

Organizational complexity arises naturally from organizational activity. Department A develops a new product that requires Department C to reschedule, rearrange and reorganize. Department B also develops a product that requires Department D to reschedule, rearrange, reassess, reevaluate, and respond. Before long, Department E arises to resolve the conflicts in Departments A through D. Soon, processes are documented, managers are trained, and line workers adjust to the new resolutions.

Then something happens to add complexity: Department A notices a slippage in revenue in their product. They write more processes, develop more marketing materials, add staff to prop up the lack of sales—they've added unnecessary complexity.

Analogy: Each of us has storage space in our homes or apartments. When we no longer desire something, we place it in storage space thinking, "I'm sure I'll need that one day." We rarely do, yet we add complexity to the storage space, preventing us from accessing critical items when we need them. We add unnecessary emotional stress, absorb precious resources, and make our lives more complicated—all because we believe (somehow, somewhere, some day) we'll need those items.

The Impact of Organizational Complexity

No organization has endless resources. There are three precious assets in every organization: human motivation, time, and cash. There are limits to all three. If we do not seek organizational simplicity, we expend grievous amounts of energy maintaining policies and procedures that mattered at one time, but matter no more!

Barriers to Organizational Simplicity

What are the barriers to simplicity? What's holding you back from making things easier, simpler (and thus, faster), more efficient, and less emotionally draining on your employees?

- A lack of managerial intent to simplify.
- A lack of understanding of organizational priorities based on the future.
- An excessive focus on innovation without a commensurate balance of simplification.
- A lack of organizational discipline.
- A lack of managerial courage to get rid of the stuff we don't need.

Future Focus

The organization that takes the time to refocus, regroup and refresh will be miles ahead of their competition. Every penny, schilling, farthing, ruble, yen or euro spent on unnecessary projects impacts everyone in your organization. People will thank you if they know you've taken the time to ensure their time is well spent.

Reframing Power
as Organizational Energy

Power. The mere utterance of the word evokes a reaction. People often have negative feelings about the word because abuses of power are familiar to anyone with even a cursory knowledge of world history. "Power" is a word with a troubled past.

It seems human beings have a strange love/hate relationship with power. Jeffery Pfeffer, in his book, *Managing with Power: Politics and Influence in Organizations*, wrote:

"It is interesting that when we use power ourselves, we see it as a good force and wish we had more. When others use it against us, particularly when it is used to thwart our goals and ambitions, we see it as an evil" *(1992, p. 16).*

And yet, power plays a key role in our organizational lives. Pfeffer writes: "Unless we are willing to come to terms with organizational power and influence, and admit that ***the skills of getting things done are as important as the skills of figuring out what to do***, our organizations will fall further and further behind" *(p. 12, italics mine).* The need for power in organizations is not likely to go away very soon, and yet the word power still causes us concern. What is power in organizations? *Power is politics.*

"Its not rocket science, its political science."

All of us have heard the phrase "Its not rocket science, its political science," by which the frustrated members of our organizations express their distress as they feel put upon by those who are the "power elite." We know organizations and groups are not immune from power conflicts, but we tend to use the euphemism *"politics"* to describe the use and abuse of power in organizations.

Why is power necessary in organizations? Pfeffer describes power as "The potential ability to influence behavior, to change the course of events, to overcome resistance, and to get people to do things they would not otherwise do." *(p. 30)*. In a nutshell, it's about getting things done through people.

Power as Organizational Direction

"If everyone agrees on what to do and how to do it, there is no need to exercise power to attempt to influence others." *(Pfeffer, p. 176)*. But we all know it's a rare day when everyone agrees on what to do and how to do it. If an organization is to get things done, it must be focused on a goal. "There are politics involved in innovation and change..." *(Pfeffer, p. 12)*. This is power of **direction**. While this can be achieved democratically, not everyone in the organization has the same perspective of the goal, and eventually the organization either gets things done or dies.

Power as Organizational Decisions

If an organization is to accomplish something, it requires some kind of structure to direct the energy flow. This is the power to **decide**. "Because the need for power arises only under circumstances of disagreement, one of the personal attributes of powerful people is the willingness to engage in conflict with others." *(Pfeffer, p. 176)*. In other words, decision-making is power. At the end of the day, whilst many get frustrated with organizational decisions, few want to carry the burden of the risks or mistakes inherent in decision-making. "Heavy is the head that wears a crown." *~Shakespeare, HENY IV*

Power as Organizational Discipline

If an organization is to work together, it requires some kind of policies to evaluate, encourage or, in some cases, eliminate those who do not choose to cooperate. This is the power of **discipline**.

Power is necessary in organizations, but it does not need to retain it's bad reputation.

Power re-framed as Organizational Energy

Power may be legitimately re-framed as organizational energy; the combined forces of human motivation driving toward complex, but achievable, goals. It is an energy source that leaders use to infuse an organization with enthusiasm, vigor, and focus, and can be used to persuade and guide. Organizational power is the energy needed to get things done.

Organizational energy increases as leaders effectively use these tools. Every organization has "power tools" that wise leaders can use to increase organizational effectiveness. Here are a few:

- **Knowing (and working with) the <u>real</u> influencers in organizations.** Every organization has people who influence far more heavily than their box on the organizational chart might lead others to believe. Wise leaders work with these influential leaders to get things done and increase organizational acceleration.
- **Building Organizational Coalitions** Coalitions are the effective development of groups of people working toward helpful achievements. Wise leaders cultivate coalitions through persistence, persuasion and passion.
- **Leading Organizational Calibration** Calibration is the work of wise leaders who draw dissimilar people together through the use of common, powerful goals. One might call it "*Unity in Diversity.*"
- **Effectively Using Existing Networks** Every organization has existing networks of people who combine their efforts to achieve organizational goals. Wise leaders understand the value of existing networks in moving things forward more rapidly. Wise leaders know those who "know" others, and work with them to get things done.
- **Valuing Natural Autonomy** People want freedom to influence decisions. Wise leaders find ways to provide freedom within the limits of organizational goals. Wise leaders also know this: "Lower level participants in organizations also have power: the power to resist or refuse the orders of their

superiors." *(Pfeffer, p. 130)*. Autonomy can mean the power to resist. Great leaders effectively bring people along without violating their freedom to choose.

- **Valuing People's Time** Never bring a blank sheet of paper to a meeting (unless, of course, you're brainstorming), but expect to adapt whatever plan you have with team input. Organizational energy comes from effectively using people's time in a way that benefits them and the organization.
- **Quid Pro Quo** Great leaders know the value of "this for that."

We want our organizations to be powerful in the best sense of the word. We want them to have energy to burn and energy to spare. Re-framing organizational power as organizational energy can change the way we view power and, in the process, change our organizations for the better.

"We" Not "Me:" Finding Unity in Organizational Diversity

Diversity as Uniqueness People in our organizational land-scapes are mapped out in many ways these days. Whether we identify someone by their DiSC profile, their Meyers-Briggs type, their Power Distance scale, their Cultural and Gender Distinctives or, most recently, by Generational Boundaries, we see much division. We seem to be splintering into smaller and smaller groupings of people through the social science that analyzes us, and through the Organizational Training that per-petuates that analysis. Whilst it is clearly valuable to under-stand distinctions, perpetuating divisions does not serve the greater cause of organizational collaboration and achieve-ment. Even Employee Engagement is about the "me," not the "we."

Over the past decades, marketers have understood the human penchant for uniqueness, and driven organizations to greater individuality in product offerings. Customer innovations are rife with the notion that people want things individually pack-aged and uniquely suited to their desires. You can get a phone in any color or style, with your own personal imprint. Social media has added to the global drive to express unique-ness. We are all individuals who want to be seen as unique.

Most recently, as I listen to conversations and workshops about *Generational Differences* (Veterans, Boomers, Milleni-als, etc.), I hear the voices of many trying to maintain their own generational ground because they identify with their group, their generation, their clan, their people; essentially, their uniqueness. They are proud of who they are because of their distinctiveness. Generational difference research is the latest in a long list of divisions analyzed and published in the past few decades.

I doubt many would argue the value of the extensive discussions about diversity in the workplace, the value of learning and respecting cultural distinctive, and the great awareness brought about through several decades of intense scholarly and managerial discussions about gender differences in the workplace. The management literature is filled with these subjects, and whole shelves of bookstores are dedicated to the *divisions* of human beings based on their individuality. There is a constant flow of research and publishing that says, "We're different." In short, we now know we are all different according to any of a number of categorizations; yet, at the same time, organizations are stressing the need for collaboration.

Opposing Organizational Forces: Individual Uniqueness and Organizational Collaboration Much of organizational life happens as a tension (not always a balance) between two opposing forces. For example, we see the tension between operations and sales, between marketing and engineering, between management and labor, between standardization and innovation, between strategy and tactics, between centralization and decentralization. These forces are likely to remain as part of organizational life.

Opposing forces create useful tensions that often (not always) yield better organizational solutions. In this case of unity in diversity, the challenge is between acknowledging our differences while still focusing on what we can accomplish together. A constant reminder of the divisions between us will not help the greater cause of organizational collaboration. The pendulum has swung very far in one direction; there should be a balance. Categorizations do not make for collaboration.

Unity in Diversity Where is the organizational unity? I have a few thoughts:

- **We are united around common deeply held human motivations.** At the foundation of life, we are all human beings with powerful capacities for speech, for work, for creativity and innovation, and for achievement. We have common and global motivations to understand and realize a purpose in life, to use our gifts in behalf of our families, and to further our own careers and skills. *We are united as a species.*

- **We are united around common organizational purposes.** Our organizations have common goals that yield benefits for *all*. Organizations that work together improve the speed of decision making, the effectiveness of solutions, quicker innovation of new products, and faster speed to market which, in turn, yields better financials that perpetuate and strengthen their longevity, providing employment for millions.

- **We are united around common achievements.** One of the greatest things to behold in our organizations is the achievement of many diverse team members working together. All who are part of major projects, new concepts, new product launches know the delight of accomplishing something together, that moment where we sense the jubilation of being part of something greater; something much bigger than our own individuality. When we accomplish the "impossible" together, there is a moment of human bonding like no other that far exceeds our unique contribution. "We" did this. "We" achieved this. "We" got the job done. "We" overcame great obstacles.

We're all in this together. Throughout the past several decades, the case has been made that we are all unique, with our unique experiences, our unique learning, our unique upbringing, our unique country of origin. That case has been made. In short, we all have a unique life history and we should be respected for our individuality. I just wonder whether all our focus on uniqueness has impeded our collective achievement. Working together is a reward that honors our individuality, while still allowing us to accomplish things we simply could not do on our own.

Hamster Wheel Projects: The Danger of Irrational Organizational Priorities

Most organizations develop initiatives every year around Strategic Plans. It's a normal, logical thing to do because it sets so many other organizational elements in motion. We have a plan, we need to staff and invest to achieve those plans. Teams are assembled, and work begins. Yet, there comes a place where we need to exercise our organizational conscience and say, "This project is not working, and even though it was a strategic initiative, we need to stop investment now." To quote Hamlet: "Aye, there's the rub."

Why do organizations continue to invest in projects even when it becomes glaringly obvious that those projects are not yielding expected ROI?   Here are some observations:

- **"Teacher's Pet" Projects:** It's someone's pet project (typically a high level executive). When an executive's ego and reputation is at stake, it's tough to discontinue the work on a lost cause.
- **"Hope Springs Eternal" Projects:** So much money has been spent to get it off the ground that people are reluctant to shut it down. *"Maybe if we just add a few more people."*
- **"Took Your Eyes Off the Ball" Projects:** In some circumstances, people aren't paying attention to the project at all.
- **"Hamster Wheel" Projects:** BAU (Business As Usual) projects prevent people from seeing the forest for the trees. "Why are you working on this?" "I don't know, we just keep working on it." Again, this is generally due to a lack of attention.
- **"Don't Bring Me Bad News" Projects:** Someone can't (or won't) believe it is failing, and will not accept failure (*Gene Krantz persona, but this isn't Apollo 13*).

Organizations cannot continue to invest in the human effort, financial costs and missed opportunities associated with projects that are not bringing in the forecasted ROI.

What to do?

While ruthlessly axing projects is nearly as deadly as ruthlessly axing people, organizations that want to succeed must be honest about failure. After honesty comes a willingness to say, "We're done with this. Let's focus somewhere else."

Why won't people do that?

- Fear that someone will be offended.
- Fear that someone's job will be lost.
- Fear that *one's own job* will be at stake.
- Uncertainty due to a lack of hard data about likely project effectiveness and ROI.
- Lack of interest.

Uncertainty about the data is the only acceptable reason for <u>caution </u>when axing a project. The others are excuses which can cause further catastrophic failures and losses in an organization. Candidly, people could be offended if you *continue* with a failed initiative and, what's worse, *many* people could lose their jobs—including you!

Sometimes, the only way to bring these issues to the surface is to bring in an outside resource to examine the details and make recommendations by taking a serious look at the initiatives you currently have underway. Are those initiatives making the best use of your resources, time, energy, and—that precious commodity—human motivation?

Cut those projects that are wasting time, and your organization—and your people—will thank you for your courage.

Why Best Practices Often Aren't

"Best Practices" often don't live up to expectations, yet we persist in the belief that they exist in some corporate domain, somewhere in the business universe. And because big corporate names are often attached to these "best practices," we associate their organizational persona with the success of the best practice they developed. We want to be like them, because we secretly believe they found the silver bullet to success.

Best Practices are the outcome of the quality movement and other corporate searches for the "Holy Grail" of business, but they don't always work out as planned. Here's why:

Every organization is different. (Am I stating the obvious? Please forgive me.) This includes the leadership, markets, employees, customers, products, services, policies, strategic direction and organizational performance at the time of the "best practice." The complexity of organizational structure makes the implementation of a "best practice" nearly impossible to achieve. A "best practice" generally arose from some organizational suffering requiring rethinking, retooling, and reappraisal. That suffering induced effort—often strenuous effort—to resolve a major issue. Without that requisite suffering, organizational bystanders may *study* a "best practice," but they will not likely be as engaged in applying the practice in their circumstance. The "best practice" we read in a polished marketing brochure may be radically different from where it started. In other words, we may not be getting the whole story.

So, what are these "best practices" good for?

The value of a "best practice" is the awareness of a different way to do things. They create an avenue for discussion that comes from outside the corporation, and are often less threatening to those who are failing to lead. In every perceived "best practice" there is an element of truth which can be applied in one's circumstance. There is always something to learn and apply; *the will to do so, however, is still the limiting factor.*

An Alternative!

Sometimes, your "best practices" are within your own walls. People within your company are doing amazing things that can change your company! *("A prophet is not without honor except in his own land ...").*

The exemplar teams within your company would benefit from the recognition you could provide by acknowledging their achievements (and just think of what that would do for Employee Engagement!).

Sometimes, just good old fashioned hard work and brainstorming can produce remarkable results within your company. Who knows? Maybe your organization will come up with the next "best practice!"

SECTION III
ORGANIZATIONAL LEADERSHIP
Tools, Techniques & Hot Spots

HOT SPOTS

181

How to Survive
Organizational Dragons

Sometimes we are placed into the care of a dragon through an organizational restructuring. Sometimes (at least once, in my case), we go to work for them *because we must slay them before we can get to the things we desire in our corporations.*

Dragons are those charming leaders who turn against you when things go sour, scream at you from the top of their lungs, and make your life a living nightmare. *Do not be fooled.* Dragons are deadly and dangerous. They walk the corridors of their perceived power (although some of them may be of little import in the grand scheme of the organization) with much aplomb and self-importance. They have the power to throw flames on the highway of your career. Having survived a few, I am sharing some strategies with you so you may endure.

To begin, one must understand that Dragons are clever. They will go out of their way to gain your trust through warm, almost personal conversations, sharing bits of their life with you until you are lulled into a sense of safety. They may even be emotional at times, exposing elements of their insecurity and personal uncertainties. *Do not be fooled!* Dragons are always at war, imagine there is a war, or want to start a war with something or someone and, in the end, they must prevail (or at least believe they have prevailed).

Dragons are protective of their domains. Anyone who has worked for a dragon knows how they must control their domain, without question. *Do not be fooled!* Working for a dragon subjects you to the danger of unwittingly encroaching on their territory. Paying attention to what they like in their domain (lair?) will save you much trouble.

You cannot overpower a dragon - you must <u>outwit</u> them.
Outwitting the dragon takes significant stealth on your part. In jujitsu fashion, you must give them the sense of control they seek, while all the while managing them toward your own ends. One way is to listen to their ranting, raving criticisms of others without challenging their thought process (trying to persuade them otherwise is a fruitless waste of time). In this way, you are demonstrating your own intellect and your mastery of their kind.

Outperforming a dragon is the second greatest of all risks. If you outperform the dragon, you will be destroyed, unless you outperform them in *their* service without ever revealing your part of the work to others. Dragons like secrecy, especially when it comes to revealing where they derive their success.

Upstaging a dragon requires planning and a careful exit strategy. If you plan to upstage a dragon, do so with the full knowledge of the danger you are courting. Once the dragon's ire is aroused it is *never* quenched, and your actions will be remembered until you are gone. Be ready to move on immediately, and have a careful plan for your exit.

Patience is the key to surviving a dragon. Remember this: dragons invariably long for greater power, greater territory, greater influence, and greater fame. You can wait them out or leave. As I wrote above, trying to fight them will only cause you harm. Work with them and protect their insecurities, and you will likely survive. I survived several dragons in my career and lived to tell this tale. You, too, can survive a dragon, but always wear your Kevlar and flameproof clothing—*you'll need it.*

⚠ Things That Buzz Can Sting: The Risks of Corporate Buzzwords

I recently had a discussion with several very bright students who challenged the word "Empowerment." *"Millennials, challenging empowerment?"* I thought to myself, *"Unthinkable! Clearly Millennials are keenly interested in sharing power and providing people with the freedom of delegation."* And yet, the discussion went on for quite a while. It is a "buzzword."

You see, their concern was the *definition* of empowerment. Each of them had a very different view of what the word meant, and some of those definitions were not positive. For some, empowerment was the idea of encouragement; for others, it was the idea that those in authority gave "permission" to be creative, and for others, it was deeply patronizing to followers as responsive to masters. In short, there was no common understanding of the term. This is not an uncommon circumstance when buzzwords are used in the world of organizations.

Buzzwords can be a sign of organizational laziness.

Tossing around buzzwords is a risky at best (and dangerous, in some circumstances). Buzzwords can reduce productivity, create confusion, and cause a loss of credibility for those that use them. I have observed that people use buzzwords in several ways:

- To sound intellectual or up-to-date; giving an air of being insightful. *(This generally happens after an executive has read the latest leadership book.)*
- To obfuscate conversation with words no one really understands.
- To add complexity, which takes people off course.

- To shorthand a conversation.
- To imply something sinister with high sounding words.
- To legitimately enhance conversation and dialogue.

For Example:

To sound intellectual or up-to-date, giving an air of being insightful.
- **"Culture"** is a glamorous, intriguing word and it has the sophisticated ring of ... well, culture! The problem is culture is often vague and difficult to pin down. Deference to culture allows those who do not want to change the ability to say *"it's a cultural issue,"* providing them an excuse to continue on with their same old practices.

To obfuscate conversation with words no one really understands.
- **"Authenticity"** is, arguably, the most overused word of our times. According to research, Millennials prioritize authenticity as a primary criteria for judging leaders and organizations, yet I wonder whether there is agreement on this term? Does authenticity mean openly sharing every ounce of one's life; wearing one's emotions on a shirtsleeve? Or does it mean clarity in speech and decision-making? Or does it mean, "I want to know everything you know so I can decide whether to stay here"? (*Can you tell - I'm looking for an authentic meaning of authenticity.*)

To add complexity which takes people off course.
- **"Leadership"** is a widely used word in organizations, which can send a conversation in a thousand directions. Without precision, this word can mean anything and everything. Leadership has been studied for over a thousand years, and the range of definitions is mind-boggling.
- **"Employee Engagement"** Although this concept has been around for over twenty years, it is not clearly understood by the masses of leaders who are the objects of employee engagement scores. Many are the times I've seen

people nod their heads during a conversation on the subject, while privately acknowledging they had no clear understanding of what was being said.

To shorthand a conversation.
- **"Career Path"** The enlightened among us know that there is no such thing (it's more like career road construction), yet conversations are sometimes cut short by saying someone needs to do such and such to benefit their "career path." Sometimes, short-handing a conversation is simply another word for lazy thinking. Buzzwords can be a sign of organizational laziness.

To imply something sinister with high sounding words.
- **"Team Player"** When used with bad intent, there is no more dangerous term in organizational parlance.
- **"Commitment"** In the mouth of the wrong leader, this word can be used as extortion; as a lever to induce people to more hours, more effort, more time away from family.

To legitimately enhance conversation and dialogue.
Some of these words can be effective, but only when they are matched to clearly understood definitions. Legal, financial, and manufacturing terms are sharply defined in organizations —why not these?

For example, we know what ROI means. Organizations define all kinds of things to ensure clarity. Why not have an organizational wide understanding, so people know what is meant by ... [fill in the blank].

A few observations on the observations:
Sharp observers of buzzword users are quick to detect the ineffectiveness of those who use them—buzzwords should be red flags to the listener. Clarification of terms is critical in organizations: saying what we really mean can put us on the path to getting things done.

The majority of these words are "people" related. They can have a powerful impact on lives and careers. They should be used with caution and clarity.

Recommendation:
Asking people what they mean when they use oblique buzz-words is a legitimate exercise in organizations. Like good science, defining terms is good organizational practice.

Things that buzz can often sting. Think about it.

The Seven Deadly Sins
of Office Politics

We hear the word "politics" a lot, but we're often unsure what that means. There are beneficial politics which must take place for an organization to succeed (building coalitions, influencing top executives, making a case for your project versus others), but being aware of these seven (I'm sure there are more) "sins" of office politics will help us all do a better job wherever we serve. Whether an individualistic culture, like North America, or a more collectivist culture, I am convinced these "sins" have serious, and sometimes dramatic, consequences.

Overreaching
Let's start with the basics. Overreaching is simply this: you're out of your depth, and you know it. What's worse is that others know it, and they will hold you to your word. They know you don't have the competence to achieve what you've espoused. They know you don't know what you're talking about. The impulse to act as if we know something can be very powerful, but it is unwise to act upon unless we can finish what we've started.

Grandstanding
I will be the first in line to say, "The only person who can promote you is you!" but illegitimate self-promotion is a dangerous action. We also call it bragging. People don't like braggarts! And when an entire team is involved, that last thing people want to hear from you is, "See what I did!"

Stepping *Over*
If there is one warning all new supervisors should know, it's this: *do not*, in any way, shape or form, step over your manager or director or VP. You may think you're smart, you may think you have the solution, but don't overstep them. This "sin" is career suicide. It generally happens because of a lack of

patience to get things done, believing one's superior is "in the way." Think again and talk with them ahead of time if you have an idea—you need them on your side!

Up Staging
While stepping over your boss is a serious matter, there is a great "sin" managers and leaders do without considering the consequences: upstaging your boss. This is, by far, one of the most deadly career behaviors you can perform. When you make them look bad, you have put your job at risk.

Inaccuracy
In my career, my greatest failure ever was providing inaccurate data to my superior. I made excuses for my failures, but it all came down to this: I cut corners, I rushed, and avoided the necessary, detailed work required to ensure the integrity of my data. Inaccuracy becomes evident very quickly to all in the room, and credibility dissipates like smoke. While I recovered quickly from my mistake, mistrust remained in my data.

Stepping On
Other managers can become victims to your ego. Here's how it happens: you're in a meeting and you want to prove someone wrong (*or worse, prove that you're right*), so you blatantly challenge them in front of their boss (or worse, their peers!) to make a point. People remember the embarrassment and shame of moments when someone stepped on them, and one day, they may become your boss. Game over.

Overpromising
When you cannot deliver what you've promised, you've increased your own stress, and you're likely to increase the stress on your team to maintain your reputation, causing your team to rebel. The impulse to act as if we can accomplish the impossible can be very powerful, but it is unwise to act upon unless we can finish what we've started.

A confession ...

Throughout my career, I've done them all ... _one time._ They were unpleasant learning experiences, and I never did them again. It was painful learning, and I offer them to you as a gentle warning: these political mistakes have consequences that aren't pretty...but that's another story for another book!

Overcoming OADD

We see it more and more and more in our corporations every working day. We see the symptoms of OADD (Organizational Attention Deficit Disorder): inability to concentrate, loss of focus, distraction, and decreased employee morale. As the pace of change and new global challenges rise, this issue will become the primary management challenge in organizations.

Sources of OADD
Uncertainty about organizational direction, along with disconnected organizational initiatives and simply too much change happening at one time, contribute to this disorder. Organizations create their own chaos through ineffective management of programs and initiatives. Organizations create their own overload.

What does it look like at the employee level?
Uncoordinated activities from multiple directions causes confusion about how to make decisions. Uncertainty is a nemesis in a corporation. People are no longer agile, they are paralyzed— especially when everything is priority #1.

The Outcomes of Organizational OADD
An organization struggling with OADD will display incomplete projects, halted growth, inefficiencies, employee frustrations, and, ultimately, loss of market share. So, what is a leader to do to overcome OADD?

The best leaders truly understand critical organizational priorities. They spend time with their managers to gain insight into the key, long term goals of the corporation—not just the strategic plan, but *the real projects and initiatives that will yield the greatest financial and organizational results*. Leaders need to clearly understand what their organizations want to achieve, irrespective of today's hot projects. There will always be hot projects. Things go wrong, but if we simply react to the things that are in our way, we lose focus and never reject unnecessary projects coming our direction.

The best leaders understand the true workload of their team. Understanding workload is sometimes a daily activity requiring a document that simply outlines the major projects and activities of the team. It is a hard discipline, but a necessary discipline. Team members can tell whether you truly understand what they're trying to accomplish, or if you're just waiting around for your next assignment. The best leaders understand the capacity of their people. People cannot work interminably without burning out, the upshot of which is loss of great employees.

The best leaders manage upwardly to prevent overload and maintain focus. It takes a great deal of managerial courage to say no. Clearly, there are many ways to say no without insulting a leader, but any manager or leader who continues to take on more and more activities without considering the effectiveness of their team is chipping away at their own foundation.

In my experience, here are the specific actions I have taken to manage past the clutter and into the heart of organizational aspirations. Ultimately, it's about the following managerial/leadership disciplines:

- **Provide maximum goal clarity**. In some ways, a lack of leadership discipline causes OADD.
- **Manage priorities.** Your team looks to you to manage the priorities and take the heat.
- **Maintain focus on your team.** What is their role in the corporation? Why do they exist? What does the organization expect them to produce? As a leader, you know the answers to those questions, and you know the powerful value of maintaining focus in the midst of chaos.

- **Stay the course to get the job done.** Sometimes you need to repeat the goals of the team until people no longer want to hear them. I've done it, and people got frustrated, but they got the job done, and they got rewarded for top performance.

On a side note, watch for the social loafers in your organization who send work your way. There is always room to be a team player on a common goal that exceeds departmental boundaries, but when one of your team members is asked to spend time on another team, ensure that their time is spent on the priorities you've set by assessing what the corporation really wants to achieve.

In the end, your success as a leader will be dramatically affected by your own disciplined management of OADD. The distractions you remove will make all the difference, *and your team will thank you.*

Organizational Collaboration:
Perspectives from Those
Who Do the Work

Why is it a challenge for people to work together? Throughout our working lives, we must join forces with people, either willingly, (as in a volunteer organization) or unwillingly (as in being put on the same team in a work environment with someone we don't like to work with). In the end, however, the goal of our time together was to advance some cause or complete a task or project. People should work together, shouldn't they? *Collaboration is a good thing.* We all know that, at least in principle. So the question is, why don't people work together like they should? Gaining an insight into this phenomenon is crucial for organizations, since often the only way to improve speed and synergy of ideas is to work together. Consultants face this dilemma every time they work with a client attempting organizational change. The literature is filled with the need for collaboration, but a discussion of why people can't seem to "get along" seems conspicuously absent, like the elephant in the corner no one wants to acknowledge.

Perhaps that is because we're all a little guilty of not working together like we should, or maybe it's because we don't like the sound of the negativity, but let's face it: this issue is an important one, so a dialogue would be valuable for us all. The speed at which change happens in organizations is a factor of mission, focus and, most importantly, collaboration. To be co-laborers means we work together to get the job done. Some of you may have seen that wonderful scene in the move *Witness*, where a barn was raised by a group of people collaborating in a greater cause that served the greater good. Their cooperation touched us all, because deep inside, we want it to be that way. We want people to work together. So why can't we all get along?

A Qualitative Study

I posed a question to multiple people, including consulting and HR professionals across a wide population, to assess why people can't seem to work together. The twenty responses are clustered around several different themes, along with some suggestions about how we might go about managing these issues to collaborate better. The sample of respondents is broad, global, and gender balanced across a wide variety of vocations. Participants were asked to complete the following open ended sentence: *People in organizations have a difficult time working together because...*

One person provided an interesting synopsis of the issue: "One could write a book or two on the subject. I will limit my answer to ten minutes. We, not "people", have a difficult time working with one another for a variety of reasons that are *complex* (involving many factors), *dynamic* (the factors interact in ever-changing ways), and often *mysterious* (unpredictable, uncontrollable, and unavoidable)."
~ *Organizational Consultant*

According to those surveyed, people in organizations have a difficult time working together for six major reasons:

1. **I'm only human!**
2. **Personality Differences and Personality Conflicts**
3. **Personal and Hidden Agendas**
4. **Perceived Fairness and Lack of Trust**
5. **Individualistic Management Practices**
6. **Inability to Deal with Conflict.**

I'll take each of these in turn, and offer some opportunities for consideration as we deal with this important issue.

I'm only human!

The first reason for our inability to work together appears to be deeply fundamental, almost as if it is in our DNA. Several respondents suggested that fear and selfishness are reasons people may not work together. For example:

"People in organizations have a difficult time working together because they feel threatened by today's highly competitive work environment, in which skills and competencies change as technology changes."
~ *Innovation and learning consultant*

"People in organizations have a difficult time working together because they are human ... and that's what happens with humans every now and again, particularly when placed in an environment where they don't choose those they are with or they spend too long with them that even the little things get annoying."
~*Consultant*

"Selfishness: I want my agenda and do all I can to make it happen. If you and I can negotiate a "win-win" deal, fine. But if we can't, it becomes difficult to work with one another. There are numerous factors relating to selfishness."
~*President of a Consulting Firm*

Opportunities for Improvement
It is unlikely we shall change the fundamentals of human nature. The literature is filled with the reality that people have fear of new things, fear of new people, and that fear and discomfort takes them out of their comfort zone, thus making it difficult to work together. As to selfishness, that is a characteristic that might be better stated as "what's-in-it-for-me?" Anyone who has worked with groups understands that American culture in particular pushes individualism, and thus fosters a refined sense of selfishness. Yet without some answer to this question, consultants and managers will find it difficult to get groups to work together. Simply knowing that these realities exist, as opposed to having some rose-colored-glasses view of how people *should* work together, will go a long way in assisting teams.

Personality Differences and Personality Conflicts

A second major reason people have a tough time working together is individual differences. This is not hard to understand. We all grow up in different environments; we react differently to different foods, music, and events. Every person has a unique life history that may match some of the vectors and tangents of the lives of others but, most of the time, we see the universe through our eyes. It should not surprise us that our individual differences should be a major factor in our inability to work together.

"...because many people have a very difficult time separating the personal from the professional ..."
~Dean of a College

"People in organizations find it difficult to work together because of the wide variety of personalities, characteristics, and opinions each member of the organization may have. Trying to put these things aside and focus in on the one common point that brings the group together is sometimes difficult to do."
~Administrative Person

"... Some are introverts, shy, have limited cognitive or emotional intelligence, dogmatic, "know it alls," lazy, have significant factual belief, attitude, or value differences, politics, ambition, unwillingness to take risks, devalue opinions and thoughts of others, are lousy communicators, poor listening skills... the list could go on for ever."
~Professor

People in organizations have a difficult time working together because...
- They are driven by different goals/objectives that may clash
- They lack emotional maturity
- They lack the interpersonal skills necessary for resolving complex interpersonal situations."
~ *Sales executive and trainer*

"More often than not, between two or more people of similar personality, two extroverted aggressive types butt heads, etc."
~ *President of a Consulting Firm.*

"Because of personality differences. Personalities which complement each other are rarely considered when work groups are chosen."
~ *Consultant and college professor.*

Opportunities for Improvement

So how do we deal with this? Getting this issue out in the open as opposed to hiding it is the right place to start. Expecting everyone to match the behavior of the leader or the leader's expectations simply doesn't make sense. Discussing differences in personality and how that can *help* the group process is of great advantage. It relieves some pressure to conform, and acknowledges that people are simply going to be different. Getting comfortable with the differences is what makes the difference! Sometimes, I think the greater diversity issue we face is not gender or race, but the broad varieties of experiences we have all had in our lives, and how they have shaped us. These things are the roots of who we are and, as we all know, they are very difficult to change. Let's face it: we are all products of years of decisions, learning, travel, and interactions with various people, and we have formulated our view of the world through our experience. Acknowledging this reality is a good starting point.

Personal—and hidden—Agendas

Here we find some of the tougher stuff. Personal agendas are always lurking in the caverns of every mind. *("Aye – there's the rub.")* Recent books on power like Kathleen Reardon's *Secret Handshake* show insight into this insidious side of human nature. Note the comments that follow:

"Hidden agendas."
~*Senior Analyst - Education & Organization Development*

"People in organizations have a difficult time working together because...they have different needs and goals. In short, what motivates each person to behave as they do may be totally different, which can lead to conflict."
~Professor New Zealand

"Ideological conflicts: What I generally refer to as conflicting perspectives related to beliefs, values, and desires. This discussion generally takes the form of what we think we 'ought' to do."
~ President of a Consulting Firm.

"We are able to see the faults and inconsistencies of others, but not our own. We are better at understanding the motives of others than we are our own. It all makes for a big mess. By the grace of God, we are able to get something done sometimes anyway."
~ Pastor

"... they come to the table with different agendas. People are held accountable for the completion of their part of the project, not the whole."
~ Training Project Manager

"Turf battles—power struggles."
~ Senior Analyst - Education & Organization Development

Opportunities for Improvement

An "agenda," at the end of the day, is really about need fulfillment, about power, about gains, about a desire to accomplish something from one's efforts, about recognition, about feeling valued, about being "heard," and about showing the world personal competence. Managers must recognize this as they assemble teams. It's the elephant in the corner that must be acknowledged. People have goals in mind, whether they take a new job or a new assignment. Personal fulfillment is to be a naturally expected undercurrent in the grand scheme of what makes people tick. People work so they can gain promotions, and the income commensurate with greater responsibility and greater position. The consultant's/manager's role here is to accept that personal agendas will always exist, but carefully construct how their agendas will drive to accomplishing something greater, and showing (really demonstrating) how putting aside their individual agendas for a greater good *is better over the long haul for everyone's agenda.*

One personal agenda that comes up again and again is the issue of competence. People want to show their competence; it's a cardinal rule of psychology, so denoting how people fit into projects and "rewarding" them for their competence in the presence of peers is a great way to provide psychological fulfillment to people, and bring them to the greater cause.

As to turf wars and power battles, the only people who can really solve that issue are leaders at the very top of the organization, through their example. That example will be pervasive in its effects, either for good or ill. People watch how top leaders sort things out; its the greater agenda, for the greater good and mission of the organization, that must be the overall focus.

Perceived Unfairness and Lack of Trust

Another key issue that arose in the research is the idea of perceived fairness. In other words, is everyone doing his or her part? Is social loafing going on? Is everyone pulling their weight? What happens at the end of the project? Will people remember the long hours I put in? The family opportunities I sacrificed? The family relationships that were strained? Am I being heard? All of these needs point to one thing: people want to be treated equitably. Note the following comments:

"People in organizations have a difficult time working together because they perceive themselves as working harder than their coworkers, and that their contribution is more important than their coworkers', which leads to resentment."
~ *Web Developer*

"People in organizations have a difficult time working together because people have different work ethics."
~ *Accountant*

"People in organizations find it difficult to work together because...they don't know their co-workers, and are very suspicious of their co-workers intentions. New people to a group also will find it difficult, since there is a natural barricade that seems to go up until the new person "proves" his worth to the group. Sometimes, there may also be the fear of infringement into one's territory—afraid that someone else will either take credit for, or undermine, the others' work."
~ *Administrative person*

"Issues of trust, more often than not caused by incongruent behavior. I say I will do something, but don't. When my espoused theory (it is important to provide timely feedback) is significantly different than my theory-in-use (I seldom actually give such feedback), people begin to view me as dishonest and lacking integrity. Trust begins to break down, so that people have a difficult time working together."
~ *President of a Consulting Firm*

"Lack of appreciation for the inclusion of all ideas and Organizational Politics."
~ *Senior Analyst - Education & Organization Development*

Opportunities for Improvement

Managers and consultants can build trust on teams through several means. Being careful how they criticize people on the team is a major issue, since one person may see this as unfair, and others may, in turn, take unfair advantage of the situation. People have a sharp and keen sense of fairness, which is rooted all the way back to their experience as children. The recognition process used in teams is also crucial to perceived fairness, whether it is the amount of time the manager spends with individuals, or how much time they spend together outside the workplace. Fairness issues must be dealt with quickly.

Delaying the resolution of such issues only breeds a greater misperception of inequity, and spurs on conversations that focus energy on fairness and not the task at hand.

Individualistic Management Practices

One pervasive issue in the study revolved around individualistic management practices. Note the following statements:

"Because of the competitive nature intrinsic to many business environments: competition for power, for advancement, for rewards, etc."
~ *Consultant and college professor*

"People in organizations have a difficult time working together because American organizations design so much of their work and rewards to emphasize individual accountability and accomplishments. These organizational designs reflect the American culture's high valuing of individuality, as opposed to group identity in all of its social institutions."
~ *Professor of Business*

"People in organizations have a difficult time working together because...the recognition/reward system supports individual accomplishment and puts employees and team members at odds."
~ *Training Analyst and Consultant*

"... because management often creates and sustains competitive, rather than collaborative, environments."
~ *Professor*

"People in organizations have a difficult time working together because...everyone looks to individual gains at the cost of overall group/organizational interests; organizational politics plays a larger part in rewards than fair evaluations."
~ *Assistant professor faculty of management studies University of Delhi India*

"Emphasis on individual contributions versus team work."
~ *Senior Analyst - Education & Organization Development*

Opportunities for Improvement

I find it interesting that a professor from India should perceive the same individualistic approach to business that we perceive in the US. We need to face the reality that people have personal life dreams and goals, which are supported by their work. To disregard this fact is ignorance at best, and stupidity at worst. People will not work for nothing. Even altruism brings people some kind of fulfillment. Having said that, there is truth to the notion that American individualism influences how people feel about accomplishments. It is so bred into our culture, that the normal way to extricate collaboration is through shared rewards and bonuses, based on the performance of the group. Until some managers understand the negativity that is bred in their organizations *through the unhealthy competition they unnecessarily perpetuate,* this notion of individualism is unlikely to change.

Inability to deal with Conflict

Although it was only mentioned once, conflict is an issue looming quietly in the background of the collaborative process. It takes skill and savvy, along with good role models, to sort out conflict. People simply don't like conflict. It is unpredictable, and sometimes flat out scary. Careers are sometimes won or lost in conflict situations.

"Most people, as sender or receiver, do not have the courage or skills to confront uncomfortable situations."
~ *Industrial Psychologist and Trainer*

Opportunities for Improvement

Dealing with conflict is a delicate matter. People's egos are at stake, along with their careers. People who are strong minded are called stubborn, and placed in that box, never to move higher up the ladder again because of a perception. Since people cannot control the outcomes of conflict, they are unwilling to engage it. Ultimately, this may be the one characteristic that separates the best managers and leaders and consultants from the mediocre, since the ability to manage conflict is crucial to getting people to "get along." In a non-profit organization that I am a part of, I recently witnessed that wounding of an ego, and how it contributed to conflict and, ultimately, the resignation of a person from the team. No matter how delicately these things are handled, conflict is about ego, pride, and all the deep, tough stuff of life. If all parties can walk away with some dignity and self-respect at the end of a conflict, we can move forward. In addition, an element of forgetfulness, along with a sense of humor, is a tool to bring resolution to difficult human situations.

A personal Observation

I believe one of the reasons people find it difficult to work together is a level and strength of vision by one high performing individual. No matter who we work with, and no matter what business circumstances we face, inevitably someone declares that they "know the way," or is relatively sure they know the way. If they do not have the patience to wait for others to catch up, or they cannot articulate their point clearly enough, they will get frustrated waiting for the rest of the team. But, in other instances, there are team members who, because of experience of having "been there; done that" or their training, or just flat out brilliance, really can see "the way things ought to be." Often, they are right! When they are part of a team, they will manifest a desire to move forward more quickly than others they perceive as laggards. The way to work with someone like this is to find out their success rate. They may truly see something more clearly than others, and using their way early in the game may save a lot of time.

Conclusions from the Study

People find it difficult to work together for many reasons. Sometimes, just being aware of these things helps us to shift into a positive direction. Helping people see a mission greater than their own agenda is a step in the right direction. Providing people with consistent feedback and constancy of purpose will also help us overcome some of the obstacles to getting along, but let's face it, from the time we're very young, we start with a self to feed, clothe, and fulfill. Those deep needs are not going away. So, the secret is to use the personal agendas of all for the benefit of the whole team. This will take work and effort, but the companies that are going to win in the next decade must make a diligent effort to solve this problem today.

What I found conspicuously absent in the responses was a mention of issues of diversity or gender inequality. While this is a small sample, and clearly not representative of all populations, it shows that the barriers of working together to get a common goal accomplished likely transcend diversity or gender, because the people who have reviewed this article also made little mention of diversity or gender. What they did say, however, was many of these issues resonated in their personal experience, whether male or female.

So let's go back to the scene in the movie *Witness*, where many individuals are working to build a barn for a fellow member of a religious group. There were some tensions between individuals, but the overall accomplishment of the group was remarkable. They built a barn, not a silo. Working together, in its best moments (even including grudging respect for other members of the team), always yields something bigger for everyone to revel in at the end of the day.

End of Section Personal Review

- **Does this Section address a part of your leadership/ management style that you need to improve on?**

Notes_____

_____

_____

_____

- **Do you need to share a chapter in this book with a colleague?**

Notes_____

_____

_____

_____

- **Does this Section address an issue that relates to your workplace?**

Notes_____

_____

_____

_____

- **Is there advice in this Section that would be helpful to implement in your workplace?**

Notes_____

_____

_____

_____

SECTION IV
PHILOSOPHY OF LEADERSHIP
Tools, Techniques & Hot Spots

TOOLS

My Philosophy of Management: High Expectations; High Rewards

Everyone wants high performing teams. *Everyone.* The books on team building and teamwork would fill a luxury liner, yet teams continue to struggle, and we wonder why. Having worked with multiple teams in complex environments, I have seen two principles work over and over again: *set high expectations and ensure high rewards.* This is the critical balance for managing teams.

Most managers are good at one but not the other. Here's what I mean:

High expectation managers demand excellence, pressure their teams for exceptional performance, and continually demonstrate that nothing but maximum output is acceptable. *That's one side of the equation.*

High reward managers like to treat people well with good pay and a nice environment, creating a sense of comfort for a job well done. *That's the other side of the equation.*

Neither of these extremes is valuable to an organization over the long haul. The high expectation/low reward managers burn people out, causing cynicism and loss of good talent. High reward/low expectation managers create a very friendly, family-like environment, but woe to them if they ask for more effort, more hours, or more commitment.

Examine your own style. Machiavelli asked, "Do you want to be liked or feared?" Neither is effective. Prefer rather to be highly respected as someone who is known to get the job done. Team members will always be skeptical of the new manager who comes in with flashy PowerPoint and a new motivational speech about greatness. They'll want to see action on your part.

Be willing to do the work. Team members are generally willing to accept a leader's initial expectations for raising the bar, but when you tell them you expect nothing less than award-winning, white-hot performance, they may nod, but they're looking right at you! They're thinking, "What are *you* going to do to help this team succeed?" and they're right to set their own expectations.

Two of my teams at a former organization won the highest award in the company. Several others won multiple awards for achievement. While I would not take credit for their outstanding work, I will offer that high expectations and high rewards made the difference in performance.

If you demand excellence (and I believe every leader should), you must be far above your team in learning, in performance, in commitment, in leading by example, and in persisting until things are done; and when your team does outrageously grand things, you need to go every inch of the way to get them maximum salary, bonuses, and whatever else is possible (or impossible!) to reward them. Then, set even higher expectations for the next time.

People develop self-respect when they achieve what was considered impossible. Some of the greatest joy in work comes from high fives at the end of a massive, ridiculously complex and demanding project. When people experience those moments, their work lives are validated. You can make that happen by setting radical expectations *and* providing exceptional rewards.

That's my philosophy of management, and I'm stickin' to it.

What are You Doing to Help Cinderella Employees?

Cinderella is a story familiar to many around the world. A young girl is swept away from a comfortable home and placed in a terrible environment where she is worked like a dog and hidden away from view. Her giftedness is known only to those who exploit her abilities, and used only to benefit those who manage her daily activities, but she remains hidden to the rest of the world.

Consider her plight: She grieves daily because of the trap she is in. She cannot escape, and her only means of reward is to work even harder. Deep inside, she knows she is smarter, more capable, and more intelligent than her taskmasters, but no one else knows. Her silly, mediocre peers enjoy the comforts of the favoritism shown by a manager who lacks integrity, and her greatest bitterness is her awareness that her overseers take credit for everything she has done, with no word of thanks, and no chance for escape. This is unimaginable desperation, but this is not mere fiction—*it happens in the work world every day*.

In your organization, you will find taskmasters who have placed team members into this "Cinderella" role. Those who do this unknowingly do so simply as a pragmatic way of getting work done: They know that John Smith can do a task better than anyone else, so they keep him in that role. This is not a bad thing, but John Smith is still encumbered by a manager who does not have John's interest at heart.

Then, there are the more sinister "stepmother" or "stepfather" types, who *willingly* hide good employees from others. They do so for many reasons:

- They are jealous of the person's abilities.
- They are intimidated by this person's skills.
- **This person is making them look really good.**
- If they lose this person, they will look really bad.
- If they lose this person, people will find out the truth about this manager/leader.

As a leader, one of your tasks is to create an environment where these employees can break out of the trap they are in. Build them up, raise them up, give them high levels of visibility—especially the very gifted ones who overshadow you—they will love you for it. When you have released an employee from their Cinderella servitude, their very freedom will energize them like nothing you've ever witnessed.

If you are one of those managers who has hidden employees and placed them in a Cinderella role, I assure you that one day, someone will find the glass slipper of evidence, *and your reputation will be damaged, if not destroyed.* That's how the story ended for Cinderella—she wins.

Take Good Care of Your
Administrative People

Ever wonder who *really* helps a company stay on track? Chief Executives? VPs of Finance? IT, Sourcing, Real Estate, or Marketing,? Boards of Directors? Researchers?

I hold a dissenting opinion on this one. I believe that good Administrative people are the structural steel of any organization. While all the other roles I listed are of utmost importance initiating action, good Admin people prevent organizations from flying apart, and here are ten reasons why:

1. They can contact anyone within seconds, providing speed of access to data, and improving decision-making.
2. They are persistent when a problem arises; they keep going until they find an answer to a question.
3. They know the calendars of top executives (and just about everyone else).
4. They can set up a recognition party in about an hour (and that includes catering!).
5. They connect people together, because they know what projects are happening in many areas of the organization.
6. They are proactive; often recommending how people can work together to coordinate activities.
7. *They follow through! They follow through! They follow through!*
8. They can work miracles to get people necessary resources.
9. They know the details: conference call numbers, meeting room names, locations, access to printers, maps, local restaurants for guests, have access to hotel accommodations (often in many parts of the globe!).
10. While they *see* the silos in the organization, *they often work across them to help the organization move ahead.*

And many times, they can fix your computer problem! They are sharp, intelligent, gifted people who have *mastered* the art of multi-tasking. While they may not be at the top of the organizational chart, they often write it, rewrite it, and publish it.

Good Administrative people are some of the hardest working people in your organization: They know what's going on, and they are worthy of recognition and rewards—take good care of them!

The Mythology of Soft Skills

Without exception, there is one phrase I react to whenever I hear it: *The people side of management requires <u>soft skills</u>*. I suppose I shouldn't react as sharply as I do, but it never fails. In my opinion, this phrase reflects a mythology.

Why do people use the term "soft skills"? Here's my take:
- Because unlike Accounting which measures numbers, there is no perfect measure of human behavior (at least, not from a human perspective).
- Because unlike manufacturing processes, such as injection molding that repeatedly produce the same parts, there is no perfect process for human behavior.
- Because there *is* no perfect method of analyzing human behavior—only statistical probabilities that give us guesses about how someone will behave and act (with the exception of parking lot behavior, which is very predictable!).

"Soft skills" implies that the people side of management is easier than welding steel beams or managing IT projects—after all, it's just a matter of influencing people, right? Nothing could be further from the truth. Human behavior is exceptionally *complex*, and *anything but soft*.

First of all, human emotion, motivation, perception, cognition, awareness, and need fulfillment combine to create the most complex (and thus the most difficult and demanding) challenges we face as managers.

Then, Group Dynamics (the interplay of groups within groups within divisions, etc.) all increase the level of management complexity a hundredfold. Organizational Behavior, Organizational Psychology, and Organizational Dynamics add yet another level of complexity for how people respond in organizational settings (Some call this "Politics").

Beyond all that, there is the issue of organizational and individual power (a separate subject unto itself—Jeffrey Pfeffer of Harvard has written extensively on the subject; see also, Robert Cialdini).

It is the multifaceted complexity of these interlocking organizational components that cause most managers to throw up their hands and say, "I can't find a formula so it must be something indefinable (in other words, a 'soft skill')" Nonsense! When power is interwoven with motivation and group dynamics to produce organizational demands on people, managers find these challenges far more complex than spreadsheets, IT coding, and engineering. People are complex!

The following quote demonstrates the complexity of managing "soft skills:" "Put simply, conflict in organizations is inevitable given that humans therein need to manage their mutual interdependence." *(Journal of Applied Psychology, November 2012, p. 1132)*

Whole Journals of research are dedicated to these topics every year—they are complex and demanding subjects. When managers, leaders, and executives step back for a moment, they all realize these elements are far more complex than figures, equations, and theorems. Working with people is hard work, but don't take my word for it: Albert Einstein reportedly said, *"I worked in mathematics, because people are too complicated,"* and Paul Allaire of Xerox said, *"The hardest stuff is the soft stuff."*

The mythology that people working with other people is a "soft skill" requires reconsideration—*don't* get me started!

Things I Learned About Management by Working With Rock Musicians

I believe everyone wants to be a rock musician. We call great sales people "rock stars" for a reason. Rock musicians have immense influence; they can have a crowd of thousands eating out of their hands, and they get perks most humans can't even dream of, including wealth (and special parking!). In some ways, I believe many people want to be musicians because musicians exemplify freedom of wide open expression, creativity, significant influence, autonomy, and the power of being valued. In some ways, musicians are a special window into humanity. They are what many people aspire to be, and so their behavior tells us interesting things about human nature.

Everyone wants to be a rock star.

I have worked with many musicians *(and I confess I am one myself!)*. I may have learned more about management from working with musicians than from classes or business projects. They are a unique breed, and their behavior provides us with special insight into the human condition. Here are a few of my observations after five decades of working with musicians (and note the similarities with business life):

You simply do not tell a musician what to do. You need to work with their natural and deep motivations for success and recognition. When everyone wants to do something different, it takes special effort to bring them together, but they will galvanize around something that promises a future payoff (specifically if they will get to showcase their talents and it includes remuneration).

Wise managers know you simply do not tell employees what to do! Working with them to engage natural motivations is a far superior way to increase performance. Get to know your people, then you'll understand how to stoke their motivational fires.

Musicians build efficacy through failure and regrouping. Musicians take a beating on their way to the top, starting with garage bands. They have to overcome awful venues with terrible lighting, sound, bad electrical outlets, dangerous travels, snow storms, and unscrupulous management. Rock and Roll is not always pretty, but the efficacy people gain from facing awful crowds builds momentum over time. Musicians have such a strong desire to gain a following and a hearing that they keep going in search of success.

Individuals and teams build efficacy through hard work and achievement. It is the leader's role to provide context and projects that will push employees into difficult areas and reward them when they achieve!

Musicians invest a lot in their craft, but expect something in return. Becoming a good musician takes a lot of self-discipline and effort—literally years of investment and pain. High levels of investment in time and energy build an expectation to be recognized. The lure of applause and the big crowd drives many to sacrifice family, friends, and sometimes health. Success can be its own addiction. Big crowds lead the musician to seek even bigger crowds. It is an endless cycle.

Musicians are heavily self-invested. Freedom in creativity is a goal of many musicians. They want to express their deepest thoughts and feelings through their craft. But creativity can lead to being very self-focused; their creativity is both helpful and harmful when self-importance leads to narcissism. Sometimes their talent does not match their ego, and they don't take feedback very well—they can be easily offended.

Employees invest time in education, training, skill building, night school, and other efforts to help organizations. They are heavily self-invested and they want something in return for what they do. Hiring managers need to pay attention to the investments people have made in their careers. Leaders must reward high levels of achievement.

Truly great musicians become humble and deeply satisfied in the joy of their craft. The great ones—those who, through suffering and struggle and hard work, eventually come to a place of contentment with the joy of their work— become immune to the approval of others. They simply play because they have mastered their craft and their confidence is off the charts (both literally and figuratively).

Your best workers come to a place where their pay is good, they like what they do, and they rarely need additional coaching. They are the masters—great leaders acknowledge their skills and expertise.

Working with *individual* musicians is a far cry from working with a *band*! The dreaded band meeting is the place where all the egos converge *(like business?!)*. It is a place where the bored don't want to discuss the mundane details of managing logistics and getting to gigs on time. It is a place where everyone has an idea of their own about how things should be done, according to their own creative impulses and views of the universe, and their own motivational desires for achievement.

Working with individuals in the corporate world is not at all different from working with people in organizations. Everyone has their own ideas and input. Great leaders galvanize them around a common goal.

The reality? When you stop to think about it, musicians are just the rest of us on stage. That's why everyone wants to be a rock star.

SECTION IV
PHILOSOPHY OF LEADERSHIP
Tools, Techniques & Hot Spots

TECHNIQUES

Why Your Best Ideas
Rarely Make it Past Your Desk

The world is filled with books, conferences, trinkets, magazines, journals, consultants, and seminars to generate ideas that will improve the bottom line. People get excited about the ideas generated through these resources, and sometimes they spring them on their unsuspecting organizations, yet the vast majority of spontaneous (even great!) ideas never make it past a manager's desk. Why?

I researched this issue by asking participants three simple questions:
1. What always goes wrong when a new idea comes your way?
2. Why don't things change in your organization?
3. What support do people need to make a new idea a reality?

Five findings emerged as I spoke with people from a wide range of organizations, organizational levels, and with varying levels of experience. Here's are five principles I've discovered:

Managerial Accountability
Many new ideas go nowhere because they are part of an endless stream of ideas that managers dream up, but rarely follow through. Simply put: employees have watched ideas flow out of reactions to problems, or discussions during a meeting, or from a passing conversation in a hallway, or at a bar after work. These reactions generally lead to enthusiasm on the part of the idea generators, which leads to action and effort on the part of the recipients. People rush to do work or come up with a plan, only to find out their managers really weren't serious, so the effort they put into the work comes to nothing. This leads to cynicism. If you've done this a lot throughout the years, don't expect people to come running toward your great idea. Your next idea will be met with a sense of *wait and see.* They really need co know you're serious. As one of my favorite

VPs used to say: *"Follow up or foul up."*

Organizational Context

A primary concern of human beings is: "Where do I fit in?"An important corollary is: "What is my role? What am I supposed to do? How will my job change?" Unless you answer these key questions, or at least provide opportunity for dialogue, your great idea will sit on your desk. People may pay lip service to your presentation, but at the end of the day, if they don't understand what is expected of them, your idea is dead on arrival. In addition, you must be able to answer the question of every three-year-old: *Why?* People need to be able to answer the question: "Why am I doing this?" If you don't give a solid, clear, and precise rationale, your idea won't make it past your desk.

Measurement

If there is no metric in place to assess progress, people will get the idea that this is a non-issue. On the other hand, if they find out that your new program or idea has some teeth in it, they'll pay attention. In other words, is someone checking to see if it's happening? In addition, if there is some peer pressure, they will normally respond in a positive way. Most importantly, design a way to show progress—people get enthusiastic when they see results. There is a deep need in human beings to close the loop on an activity. They need to know whether their efforts made a difference.

Training

Setting expectations for an idea is one thing; preparing people to do something new is an entirely different matter. Managers fail here because they expect people to just jump in and change without the requisite learning. They expect people to come up to speed within seconds, when it may take a few weeks or months to become skillful at a new activity. Without proper training, people will not be confident with the new program or idea. When they're not confident, they'll back away and not support the project. Why? *Because they will feel incompetent, and no one likes to feel incompetent.* If you put an idea in place without training those who must implement the change, you can plan on failure.

Support

So, expectations have been set and training has been conducted, but even with all that effort to introduce a new idea, things still go wrong! Organizational change is a multivariate activity; in other words, no matter how much you anticipate issues and develop backup plans, sometimes things don't work. The effective manager will have one more step of support to manage the project if things go wrong. Remember: early in the game, people aren't comfortable with the change, so they can't make adjustments on the fly. In psychological terms, they are not at a tacit level of undemanding. They need backup because the change hasn't become part of their lives or part of the culture yet.

You have great ideas—every leader and manager does—but the idea is not enough. These five actions are critical if you want your idea to become reality.

Why Authority Will Remain a
Critical Element in the Future

As a teacher of graduate students, many of whom are Millennials, I hear the desire for a world where power and authority no longer exists; a world where all voices are equal, and where collaboration rules the day. I listen to students and younger workers, and I hear a heartfelt desire for erasure of power distance. There is an unspoken belief that we will all, somehow, work together better without levels of authority; we will get things done without recourse to a hierarchy, but I believe the anticipated demise of authority in the workplace is a bit premature for several reasons:

The discipline required to achieve a group goal requires structure, and with structure comes authority. To accomplish organization goals, the human motivation of autonomy must be balanced by a framework of order. Power balance has been the pursuit of humanity for centuries. The desire for a world of zero power distance is the history of the world. Think about it: someone is either in power, control, or authority, or they are *resisting power, control or authority.*

Without a balance of organizational structure (e.g. hierarchy) in the workplace, autonomous humans may come up with wonderful ideas, but it is unlikely they will develop into something sustainable, because to build something sustainable requires a great deal of give and take. The discipline required to achieve a group goal requires structure, and with structure comes authority; *there is simply no way around it.*

Legitimate authority is ... Legitimate. Authority is earned through experience, time, pain, pressure and achievement. It is ludicrous to think that the fresh face of a college graduate who just walked into the door at a corporation carries the same authority as the individual who has been there for twenty years. Although there are those who might argue, "Well, there's a difference between time in a job and experience", I would answer yes, but ... experience in an organization includes the time in the trenches, building relationships, getting to know who does what, and learning the culture. Time in a role does matter, because experience is cumulative.

The pain and struggle of work and achievement also adds to legitimate authority. The "new kid on the block" does not have the same level of authority as the person who has struggled, failed, and achieved in an organization. Its not logical to even imagine they are on the same level. Even the most open-minded employee will still have a sense that they've earned a place in an organization through time, and the place they've earned demands some level of respect.

Everyone is not equal in the workplace. Voices are important, *but not all voices are equal*. Ultimately, even with the most collaborative consensus, someone must make a call; a decision. In that moment, all voices are no longer equal. Someone takes the leadership role and owns the responsibility for the outcomes of a decision; for if no one owns the outcome, no one is responsible for anything. The business world simply cannot function that way.

Should we listen to the voice of the newcomer? By all means. Perhaps they have something big to offer. But will they have the wisdom built by experience in an organization? Not at all likely.

Abuses of authority are still wrong but authority will remain. We react to authority, because we fear abuse. Abuses of power are unacceptable anywhere at any time, but the proper use of authority is essential for organizational effectiveness. It will be a part of organizations for the foreseeable future, and that's a good thing.

SECTION IV
PHILOSOPHY OF LEADERSHIP
Tools, Techniques & Hot Spots

HOT SPOTS

Intimidating Menace
or Intense Management?

In our politically correct culture (I am an American), we have developed a low tolerance for anything relationally unpleasant. In our quest for reducing emotional turmoil, we rename conflict arrogance, we rename organizational pressure and intimidation, and one of the latest trends across all manner of workplaces is calling out "bullying." Do I deny there can be such a thing as bullying in the workplace? No. I've seen it and experienced it, but I offer that it is rare (though, when present, it is awful). Yet, I am concerned that we confuse intense management with intimidating menace. *They are not the same.*

The road I've walked.
As someone who plied his skills in the workplace for over forty years, I have met all sorts of leaders, ranging from hopelessly ineffective to incredibly effective. Some were pathetic pencil pushers who maintained jobs by longstanding, high-level connections they held within companies (a.k.a. old friends who got promoted). Their emotional abuse was their bureaucratic mindset that prevented them from making decisions or "going to bat" (American baseball phrase for advocacy) for their people. Others were *true* despots and tyrants; narcissistic maniacs who frightened people and were occasionally physically abusive (yes, I personally experienced that). A much larger group, however, were leaders who had an intensity about them, but who I would never classify in terms of emotional abuse or bullying. These leaders pushed me to places *I did not want to go*, but I never felt abused in any way. They are the leaders I still think of today when I reflect on major organizational, career, and life achievements. They knew how to get the job done.

Where there's an issue, we'll take it to extremes.
In our day of internet transparency and a heightened sense of

awareness about these sorts of things, we've become very sensitive to leadership quirks that may seem too intense for our liking. HR teams use the bullying framework to hunt down abusive leaders, sometimes without a clear sense of what they're trying to accomplish. I'm opening this conversation to offer an arena for dialogue around the topic, because I fear that confusing intense management with intimidating menace may not only weaken our organizations, but do something much worse: cause <u>effective</u> leaders to back away from applying the intensity which is necessary to get things done, out of fear of reprisal and accusations of <u>bullying</u>. In short, enervating the very leaders in need of support.

Bullying vs. Intense Management

Bullying is the direct physical, verbal, emotional, or financial abuse of someone. These things happen in the workplace— I've witnessed them and been a direct object of them. These leaders are cruel, narcissistic, prone to outbursts of untamed anger, not averse to public intimidation and humiliation of employees and, in my opinion (and the opinion of experts in psychology), likely beyond redemption of *any* sort (90% of narcissists never recover), yet they often maintain roles because of their short term "effectiveness." Their motto is: *"Ignore the damaged employees—just get the job done,"* and that means they behave with no sense of respect for team members, no gratitude *("Its' your job!")*, and no inkling of personal investment in the future of their team members. If you work for one of these leaders, you either have to determine to outlive their tenure or leave. There is no humane in-between.

Intense management, on the other hand includes sharp focus, demand for excellence, willingness to engage in conflict and debate, willingness to apply significant pressure to get a job out the door, and the courage to ask employees to go the extra mile and put in more time, even when they're already exhausted. I have learned that these leaders are not necessarily emotionally invested in their people, *per se*, but they are invested in the grand products of achievement that will benefit the organization and everyone in it. Some are emotionally distant, some are emotionally connected and ebullient, but all are focused on the collaborative output of people working together. They like getting the job done. They are not, however, bullies in any sense of the word. Those who see them as bullies may be in need of a backbone, or an awareness of their own lack of motivation!

Here's the catch: When the job is done, *these* leaders are very often the first to thank their teams, to recognize them, to brag about them, and to reward them. *Rarely do these leaders draw any attention to themselves.* The second catch is this: these leaders and managers are more than willing to walk the road *with* their teams, setting the pace through example and personal investment of time and energy, showing and leading the way, not as an observer, but as a participant. If you work for one of these leaders, consider yourself blessed. You will learn much, you will become a better leader yourself, and your career will accelerate. Your exhaustion will turn to exhilaration.

A politically incorrect observation: My four decades of experience has taught me that bullying is gender, age, and race agnostic. Having spent a great deal of time with experts in psychology the past few years, I have come to learn that bullying is a human nature/personality issue. It looks a lot like self-serving, ego-invested narcissism. History has shown us what these people are: tyrants. We know them when we see them, and when we meet them. They are uncaring and insensitive maniacs that must be purged from the ranks of our organizations by other leaders who know the damage being done.

The important lesson: If we confuse these two types of leadership and management, we lose. If we cannot mentally separate intensity from intimidation, we're lost. They are not the same. Our organizations need intense, focused managers, and we need to step up and follow them.

Organizational Mythology: Leaders are Made, Not Born

I recognize this topic has some history, and for the sake of discussion, argument, and good old-fashioned debate, I'll share why I reject the idea that leaders are made and not born.

While leaders can change over time and become better at leading, I reject the idea that all leaders are made, not born. Some people have "it." Whether in music, art, education, scholarship, research, athletics—you name it—some people have "it." Even primary school children demonstrate varying levels of leadership skill—Olympians are another example.

Great leaders have "it." They instinctively know how to lead. They understand the power of anticipating risk and danger; they can martial team members together under a common banner; they demonstrate professionalism and "presence" in the face of setbacks and hardships, and they have a passion to continually improve their skills. Leadership is a set of skills in one's nascent managerial DNA, waiting for the right time or situation to present itself.

The demands of leadership distinguish real leaders from wannabes. The skills of leading–coordinating multiple competing egos, ensuring achievement of a major goal by influencing people who do not report to you, and taking the heat for things that go wrong—is an ominous responsibility requiring emotional stamina, confidence (not ego), and plain old-fashioned skill that all do not have.

Assumptions behind the statement, "Everyone is a leader:"
- The self-esteem movement has taken its toll on common sense. There is a veiled political correctness in the idea that *everyone can be a leader*. It sounds like this: "Let's

have everyone believe they can be a great leader, *so no one is left out.*"
- We are told that we may injure someone's feelings by telling them, "You don't have the right stuff to lead."
- There is a corporate belief that, in the right circumstances, anyone can "lead."
- The prevalence of corporate graffiti designed to build employee morale with signs like "We are all leaders." (This practice normally has the opposite effect, and leads to less leadership, but more cynicism.)

There are some fundamental problems with the notion that all leaders are made ...

- **Many folks flat out don't want to lead**—it's scary, takes too much time and too much effort, and carries too much risk. They would rather complain about the leaders they have than become a target for criticism and rejection. If you told them they were leaders, they would likely reject your appeals.
- **Some people try to lead, and fail miserably.** Many people who have been told they could lead turn out to be miserable failures, seriously impacting many people. You've seen them. It's tough on them, those they lead, and their organizations.
- **Worst of all - some people in leadership roles simply cannot get the job done.** While they may have the title, they do not have the skills and proficiency of leadership. The corporation knows it, the people know it, peers know it, and subordinates know it. Yet, these "non-leaders" continue to wreak havoc because of their titles and span of control.

In our times, there is a serious and profound need for real leadership. Let the leaders arise, but let's not make the mistake of assuming that everyone can lead. It's a mythology that carries too much risk for our teams and our organizations.

Want to Think Outside the Box? Stop Putting People in Them!

Like so many business clichés, the phrase "think outside the box" is overused. It is a phrase like "low hanging fruit," whose days are numbered and over, and yet, the phrase "think outside the box" caused me to reflect about something critical: *We put people in boxes all the time.*

Putting Dr. Bohn in a Box

If you just met me, you'll immediately make some conclusions about me based on what you've read and what the media has told you about people like me (White. Male. Baby Boomer). The social pressure is so powerful, it's almost impossible not to make those assumptions; and, based on those assumptions, you'll work with me in a certain way, until my behavior proves you wrong—and maybe even then, you'll retain a bias. What's worse is you may look for elements of my behavior that *confirm* what you believe to be true of me, whilst dismissing other elements that don't fit the profile. I experienced that while I was doing my doctoral studies; "capitalist pig" was one of the phrases, I recall. It was instructive for me to have that experience, but it was not an accurate appraisal of my life.

The truth is this: I cannot help being who I am...*on the surface.* My place in time, my gender, my race, even my location were all outside my control the day of my birth. The same is true of everyone else on this planet. We are who we are. The image, however, belies fifteen years of night school I labored through to become educated, my early life experiences (including some rather formative experiences as a young man spending summers in the inner city), my experience with a handicapped sibling, and the role models of very strong women. Those experiences are all invisible to you, but they have significant bearing on my life; and, because of those experiences, I don't fit the implications of those boxes. Now, with the advent (proliferation!) of generational studies, *we have more boxes than ever*, and those boxes create assumptions and preconceptions that can cause us to act in false ways toward others.

Human beings defy surface description. We are not one thing; *we are not the labels assigned.* My father was a blue collar man who could not sign his name, and his ethic informs my life, but you wouldn't know that by looking at my profile picture. The suit, tie, and white shirt say something that is only true on the surface, but the image is not the man.

Think about the boxes that we have created throughout the past several decades: Myers-Briggs inventories, DiSC profiles, categories of generational differences, diversity studies and gender research—you name it. We've all read it and, in some ways, we've become victims of our own research. Through our focus on individual differences, we have created the very anger we find ourselves in.

I've seen situations where, based on things person A has read or heard, and based on person A's experience with person B, who may have demonstrated the expected set of behaviors, expectations were set that *all people like person B* would act the same way. But that logic is in error, because it ignores the very individuality people argue for. I am not person B. I am person C.

The impact to our work life, and Beyond:
I am convinced that the false assumptions we hold about co-workers (the boxes) may be the greatest threat to effective communication, and when communication fails, organizations slow down, become ineffective, and waste time on non-essential problems. I believe the great strides that have been made in diversity and gender balance in the workplace can be muted by a continuing emphasis on differences.

But individuality is important—respect me as I am!

People want to be seen as individuals, certainly. They say: "But what about my culture, my upbringing, my history, *my* identity? Show me some respect!" An individual's history, culture, geography, education, and upbringing all contribute to our uniqueness as individuals. Our differences, uniqueness, and individuality all make for rich conversation and dialogue; yet today, the lens seems to be focused so sharply on the boxes that we fail to see the commonality of life, and thus it is easy to find "slights" in so many areas.

If it is not rational to bring all of our work life to our personal life, is it rational to bring all of our personal life to our work life? What about common humanity and common goals?

I'm afraid we've lost the ability to see each other through the fundamental lens of humanity. Instead, we've whittled away the deeper common traits of cognition, emotion, motivation, desire for achievement, a desire to live a decent life, and desire to accomplish big things, and replaced it with surface beliefs that mean very little.

Sports teams may be the best model for us to use to consider the common goals we can achieve by using our skills, abilities, and talents without putting people into boxes. When I work on a team, I want creativity, intellect, skill, competence, and experience, *no matter what package it comes in!*

Want to think outside the box? Stop putting people in boxes! In the workplace, we do have common ground and a common focus, irrespective of our individual traits or identities. People are willing to share knowledge and skill to accomplish a goal together for better working conditions, to make a better use of our time, and to improve the ways we can work together. We have deep, common interests in solving organizational and global problems, so let's put our boxes away and focus on what we can do together.

The Academy and Business: Wary, but Necessary, Partners

"I've looked at life from both sides now," sang Judy Collins several decades ago. As a business leader who earned a doctorate whilst working in the real world, I too have looked at life from both sides now. Specifically, I've seen how the Academy (Higher Education) views business, and how business views the Academy. Fascinating to me is the wariness on both sides of this critical, and ultimately necessary, partnership. The Academy and Business are two very different worlds with different cultures, different speeds and different approaches to leadership.

The Academy is wary of Business. I spent hundreds (thousands?) of hours working through my degrees, and came to understand how business is viewed within the walls of Academe. In short, except for (logically) the business schools, the Academy is wary of business. Businesspeople are the unwashed and, in some cases, "those people tainted by capitalism." Or how about, "Business people have fallen from the pure faith and are only profit-grubbing scoundrels." *Yes, I've heard those words.*

Business is wary of the Academy. Businesses see professorial types and sometimes think to themselves: "You don't know what you're talking about," or "You don't live in the real world." I know. I've done it. I've seen professors of management who had never managed anything or anyone.

At stake for all businesses is the day-to-day pressure of making profit. Businesses are not employment agencies that simply exist to allow people a place to work—they must make a profit to stay afloat. It is easy to fall into the trap that says: "People in education have no idea how hard it is to keep this business running." Businesses run at a breakneck pace, whereas education can be (and often must be) a bit slower.

The three letters "Ph.D." behind my name were *not unwelcome*, but also not welcome in some of my former roles. I confess, there was probably an element of ego involved, because high level leaders are not fond of people with titles that outrank them. Probably toughest of all is the situation where an academic consultant walks in, says things that employees have said for years, and gets paid a handsome fee— without having to ensure the effectiveness of the recommendation.

The Academy needs a partnership with Business. The Academy needs business for funding, for academic projects, for research, and—drum roll—students! The applied outcomes of research flow very naturally into business, whether the social sciences, customer experience, leadership, engineering, manufacturing, innovation, and on and on. Taking real research into the real world is a wonderful thing. To do that, however, requires a trusting partnership.

Business needs the Academy for research, for invention, for great employees, and for cutting edge knowledge. Research is a far superior way to develop employee training, leadership skills, and other key managerial needs. Leadership training, for example, built from hard-edged, statistically validated research is superior to much of the off-the-cuff literature penned by so called experts that fills bookstore shelves.

What can be done? As with all wary partnerships, small steps are a good idea. Publishing successes helps to demonstrate how the partnership works. The relationships between top leaders is, of course, extremely important in developing a partnership.

I attribute much of my personal success in business to the research and learning I gained in the academy, but the learning would have remained in books and dusty shelves if I had not had the opportunity to put it to work, at work.

End of Section Personal Review

- **Does this Section address a part of your leadership/ management style that you need to improve on?**

Notes_____

_____

_____

_____

- **Do you need to share a chapter in this book with a colleague?**

Notes_____

_____

_____

_____

- **Does this Section address an issue that relates to your workplace?**

Notes_____

_____

_____

_____

- **Is there advice in this Section that would be helpful to implement in your workplace?**

Notes_____

_____

_____

_____

The Bottom Line

The ultimate measure of leader effectiveness? Bringing people together to achieve results.

We all seem to know what we want. Of late, we have more and more people seeking the common good of the world, whether it is through energy efficiency, good use of natural resources, sustainability of the planet, improved healthcare for all, and so much more. In short, people know what is important and what is good. We know the type of future we want for ourselves, our children, and generations to come.

In *business*, we see the need to resolve chronic issues, invent new technologies, provide innovation, design new programs to improve employee welfare—the list is endless. In *education*, we want improved performance and equity; in *government*, we want services that can support our national and international interests. In volunteerism and *non-profits*, we want people to engage in and support causes they believe in. So far, so good. We understand what we want to achieve—but how do we do that?!

Leadership is not merely some grand set of carefully crafted motivational speeches. Leadership is that powerful set of skills which provides a motivational focal point for all kinds of people to take part in achieving something really big, but achieving these lofty goals requires more than aspiration; it requires the critical leadership skill of bringing people together. Influencing people to work together is a major leadership challenge.

How do leaders bring people together?

- It means *clear articulation of an end state*: Did we show people where are we going together?
- It means *collaboration*: Did we get people to work together?
- It means *knowledge sharing:* Did we get people to relinquish control of their prized learning in behalf of others?
- It means *staying the course until aspiration became realization.*
- It means *careful negotiation of alliances and interests.*
- It means *helping people understand the limits of resources.*
- *It means these things, and so much more!*

Some caveats about bringing people together:

- *It does not mean everyone will be emotionally invested in all team members.* Bringing people together to achieve something is not "Kumbaya," where we all hold hands and sing songs of peace and tranquility. In fact, it may be just the opposite. The issue for the leader is to accept emotional frustration in the face of the larger achievement, whilst still keeping people engaged.
- *It does not mean everyone was friends when the project was complete.* It does mean everyone had some voice, some influence, some impact on the outcome. *Leaders can make that happen.*
- *It does not mean everyone was happy with the final outcome.* It does mean that people had to give up some things to get some things; it means people had to take a back seat to the bigger picture; it means people may need to wait another day to get what they want. *Leaders can make that happen.*
- *It does not mean people will share the same personal, political, creedal, or social values! This is a critical matter in bringing people together.* The goal; the collectively pursued achievement is the overriding and guiding factor—

not the individual values, frameworks or histories of the people working together. *Leaders can make that happen!*

Knowing what we need to do and doing it are often two *very* different things. With all we know about leadership, what is it that prevents us from bringing people together? Why can't leaders bring people together to get stuff done? I see three major issues:

The leadership failure of *mission corruption (Don't steal my efforts for your designs!)*. Bringing people together under one espoused idea, only to reframe and redirect the idea for the leader's benefit and glory, does not lead to collective achievement.

The leadership failure of *focus* corruption *(Don't change course on me!)*. When the focus of the end goal becomes something other than initially intended, people will back away.

The leadership failure of a *lack* of *process for collaboration (Don't make me spin my wheels!)*. Sometimes, the problem of bringing people together is simply a lack of a structured process. Disorder doth not create cohesion! People need to see some kind of progression to know that their efforts are making an impact.

The bottom line: What are you doing to bring people together?

SELECTED BIBLIOGRAPHY

Anderson, Erika. "Why Top Talent Leaves: Top 10 Reasons Boiled Down to 1." Web blog post. *Forbes*. Forbes Company. 18 Jan. 2012. Web. 18 Jan. 2012.

Bandura, A. 1980. "Gauging the relationship between self-efficacy judgment and action." *Cognitive Therapy and Research*, 4(2), 263-268.

Bandura, A., Adams, N. E., Hardy, A. B., & Howells, G. N. 1980. "Tests of the generality of self-efficacy theory." *Cognitive Theory and Research*, 4, 39-66.

Bandura. A. 1986. *Social Foundations of Thought and Action*. Englewood Cliffs, NJ: Prentice Hall.

Bandura, A. 1993. "Perceived self-efficacy in cognitive development and functioning." *Educational Psychologist*, 28(2), 117-148.

Bandura, A. 1997. *Self-Efficacy: The Exercise of Control*. New York: W. H. Freeman.

Bandura, A. 1998. "Personal and collective efficacy in human adaptation and change." In J. G. Adair, D. Belangger, & K. L. Dion, (Eds), *Advances in psychological science*: Vol. 1. Personal, social and cultural aspects. Hove: UK Psychology Press.

Bandura, A. 2000. "Exercise of human agency through collective efficacy." *Current Directions in Psychological Science, 9,* 75-78.

Bohn, J. G. 2010. "Development and Exploratory Validation of an Organizational Efficacy Scale." Human Resource Development Quarterly, vol. 21, no. 3, Fall 2010 © Wiley Periodicals, Inc. Published online in Wiley Online Library (wileyonlinelibrary.com) • DOI: 10.1002/hrdq.20048

Bohn, Dr. Jim. 2015. *Architects of Change: Practical Tools to Build, Lead and Sustain Organizational Initiatives* CreateSpace.

(Bohn 2015)

Brooks, S. & Saltzman, J. 2012. "Why employee engagement is not strategic." *People and Strategy*. Vol. 34, (4).

Buckingham, M., & Coffmann, C. 1999. *First, Break All the Rules. What the World's Greatest Managers Do Differently.* New York: Simon & Schuster.

Church, A. 2013. "Engagement is in the eye of the beholder." *OD Practitioner*, 45, (2).

Denison, D. R. 1990. *Corporate Culture and Organizational Effectiveness.* New York: John Wiley & Sons.

Eisenberg, Eric M., Goodall, H.L., Trethwey, Angela. 2009. *Organizational Communication: Balancing Creativity and Constraint.* Bedford/St. Martin's

Fornal. P. 2002. "Developing and sustaining a high performance organizational culture." *SHRM Information Center*.

Gelfland, M., Leslie, L., Keller, K., & de Drue. 2012. "Conflict cultures in organizations: How leaders shape conflict cultures and their organizational-level consequences." *Journal of Applied Psychology. November 2012, Vol. 97, (6) 1131-1147.

Gist, M. 1987. "Self-efficacy: Implications for organizational behavior and human resource management." *Academy of Management Review*, 12, 3, 472-485.

Hagman, B. & Chartrand, J. 2009. *Trends in Executive Development*. EDA Pearson.

Howell, W., & Dipboye, R. 1982. *Essentials of Industrial and Organizational Psychology*. Homewood, IL: Dorsey Press.

Katz, D., & Kahn, R. 1978. *The Social Psychology of Organizations*. New York: John Wiley & Sons.

Kotter, J., & Heskett, J. 1992. *Corporate Culture and Performance*. New York: Macmillan.

Kozub, S., & McDonnell, J. 2000. "Exploring the relationship between cohesion and collective efficacy in teams." *Journal of Sport Behavior*, 23(2), 120-129.

Larson, C., & LaFasto, F. J. J. 1989. *Teamwork: What must go right; What can go wrong*. Newbury Park: Sage.

Lee, K., & Allen, N. J. 2002. "Organizational citizenship behavior and workplace deviance: The role of affect and cognitions" *Journal of Applied Psychology* 87 : 131-142. doi: 10.1037/0021-9010.87.1.13.

Maddux, J. 1995. *Self-Efficacy Theory: An Introduction*. In J. Maddux (Ed.), *Self-efficacy, adaptation and adjustment: Theory, research and application* (pp. 3-33). New York: Plenum Press.

Organ, D.W. 1988. *Organizational Citizenship Behavior: The Good Soldier Syndrome.* Lexington, MA: Lexington Books.

Petitta, L. & Borgogni, L. 2011. "Differential Correlates of Group and Organizational Collective Efficacy" *Journal of European Psychologist.* Vol. 16, no. 3. 187-197, doi: 10.1027/1016-9040/a000035

Podsakoff, MacKenzie, Paine, and Bachrach. 2000. "Organizational Citizenship Behaviors: A Critical Review of the Theoretical and Empirical Literature and Suggestions for Future Research." *Journal of Management* 26-3: 513-563. doi: 10.1177/014920630002600307 .

Riggs, M., Warka, J., Babasa, B., Betancourt, R., & Hooker, S. 1994. "Development and validation of self-efficacy and outcome expectancy scales for job-related applications." *Educational and Psychological Measurement,* 54(3), 793-802.

Senge, P. 1990. *The fifth discipline: The art and practice of the learning organization.* New York: Currency-Doubleday.

Shamir, B. 1990. "Calculations, values and identities: The sources of collectivistic work motivation." *Human Relations,* 43(4), 313-332.

Shea, G., & Guzzo, R. 1987, Spring. "Group effectiveness: What really matters?" *Sloan Management Review,* pp. 25–31.

Zaccaro, S., Blair, V., Peterson, C., & Zazanis, M. 1995. *Collective Efficacy.* In J. Maddux (Ed.), *Self-efficacy, adaptation and adjustment: Theory, research and application* (pp. 305-327). New York: Plenum Press.

Dr. Jim Bohn

Serving in a variety of roles in the corporate world since 1973, Dr. Jim Bohn has personally lead the transformation of multiple, underperforming teams to achieve award-winning levels of success.

After several decades with a Fortune 100 Company, Dr. Bohn launched a Change Management and Organizational Transformation Practice called ProAxios.

Dr. Bohn has personally led significant Change Management projects, including IT implementations, mergers, and reorganizations, in roles ranging from the shop floor to design, and from engineering to sales and service, along with global experience in change and operations.

Dr. Bohn taught Organization Development at the University of Wisconsin's LUBAR School of Business, Business Ethics and Strategy at Concordia University, and Leadership and Organizational Behavior at Marquette University. Deeply passionate about learning, developing, and practicing organizational research in the context of change, Dr. Bohn is a Master Facilitator, and has led hundreds of workshops with audiences ranging from frontline mechanics to Senior Vice-Presidents in the Fortune 100.

To learn more about Dr. Bohn, go to: http://proaxios.com/

Twitter: @DrJimBohn

Made in the USA
Middletown, DE
30 June 2019

THE NUTS AND BOLTS OF
LEADERSHIP
Getting the Job Done

Dr. Jim Bohn

The Blue Collar Scholar

A Companion Book to *Architects of Change*